MW01078150

In case of loss, please return to:

_____

_____

_____

_____

As a reward: $_____

Hello
my name is

Healed

THIS

LESSONS FROM JAMES

CHANGES
EVERY
THING

BEN STUART

Published by LifeWay Press® • © 2013 Ben Stuart • Reprinted 2015

ISBN 978-1-4158-7968-9 • Item 005560879

Dewey decimal classification: 227.91
Subject heading: BIBLE. N.T. JAMES--STUDY \ CHRISTIAN LIFE \ SOCIAL SKILLS

Cover design by Lauren Randalls Ervin

To order additional copies of this resource, write to LifeWay Resources Customer Service; One LifeWay Plaza; Nashville, TN 37234-0113; fax 615.251.5933; phone toll free 800.458.2772; order online at *www.lifeway.com;* email *orderentry@ lifeway.com;* or visit the LifeWay Christian Store serving you.

Printed in the United States of America

Groups Ministry Publishing • LifeWay Resources
One LifeWay Plaza • Nashville, TN 37234-0152

TABLE OF CONTENTS

ICON LEGEND

 Things to listen to

Things to watch

 Fun facts and useful tidbits of information

Digging deeper into study concepts

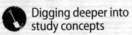 On the Web

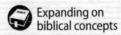 Expanding on biblical concepts

ABOUT THE AUTHOR
BEN STUART

My name is Ben Stuart. I live in College Station, Texas, with my wife, Donna, and our daughter, Hannah. I grew up in Houston and attended Texas A&M University. I received a Master of Theology from Dallas Theological Seminary. I am the executive director of Breakaway Ministries, a non-denominational, weekly Bible study for college students at Texas A&M.

In college I ministered as chaplain of a Christian fraternity and became involved in a local church. Immediately after college, I served as youth pastor for a church plant in Spring, Texas. When I first arrived there, I had one student in the youth group. It was a truly humbling, nurturing experience as God molded my heart for discipleship and evangelism.

I left my job in Spring to become a full-time seminary student, never expecting that God would take me and my wife to another full-time ministry position within a year. We prayerfully decided to accept the offer to move to College Station and for me to become the new director of Breakaway Ministries while I finished my seminary degree on the side. Having now lived in Bryan/College Station for eight years, we love these Aggie students like our own children and are constantly reminded of the kingdom value of investing in college students during this pivotal time in their lives.

In our free time, Donna and I love watching movies, hanging out with our baby girl, and attending Aggie sporting events!

This study began as a series of messages I gave at Breakaway one semester. The hope in writing this study is to provide a resource that will allow you to dig deeper into God's Word during your own personal time of study. James is a great book of the Bible because it covers so many aspects of the Christian life. As you begin this study, my hope for you is that you would see Jesus and that, through walking in closer fellowship with Him, you will be transformed.

INTRODUCTION

A LIFE CONSISTENCY

When I first read the works of the modern atheists, I anticipated encountering an intimidating display of cold, hard logic. What I discovered was quite the opposite. The modern atheist does not reason; he yells. He does not seek to refute Christianity but to berate and destroy it. Why so much anger? Because behind a thin veil of argumentation, lies a heart that has been deeply wounded by someone who claimed to be Christian but did not act consistently with his or her beliefs. Hypocrisy fuels their rage.

While many of their arguments are unfair, the perception is having an impact. Polls in the United States show a steady distancing of younger people from affiliation to any religious institution. While there are many factors that can contribute, one stands tall above the rest: disillusionment. They do not see the power of the gospel manifested in the lives of professing saints. My brothers and sisters, this should not be.

Enter James. He has no problem calling us out on conduct that is inconsistent with our convictions! James wants the way we live to fit the truth we believe.

The world desperately needs Christians whose actions match their convictions. A young generation is rising up, and they need to see the power of the gospel working its way out into our everyday lives. James will get us there. But be warned, everything is on the table. James will call you to evaluate the way you deal with hardship, handle money, use your words, and plan your future. But if we let him in, his letter has the potential to grant us an incredible gift: integrity. We have the potential for our outside to match our inside, our activity to match our God-given identity.

THE WORLD DESPERATELY NEEDS CHRISTIANS WHOSE ACTIONS MATCH THEIR CONVICTIONS.

For those who worry that James may make us legalists who try to follow an endless list of rules, do not fear. The brother of Jesus does not advocate throwing a garment of religious activity over an unconverted heart. Rather, he will call for the Christian to live out what he already has. When the gospel lands in the human heart, we cannot stay the same. James simply wants to expedite the process of renovating us from the inside out.

The gospel moves into our hearts like my wife moves into a new home. When she arrives, walls get demolished, wiring is torn out, light fixtures are trashed, and flooring is ripped up. No room is safe! But eventually holes are also patched, new wiring is woven in, superior lighting is put in place, and sturdier floors are laid down. Beauty replaces the ashes. The chaos leads to life.

This is what happens when the gospel of Jesus Christ takes up residence in a human heart. When the Spirit of God moves in, a massive renovation takes place! We cannot stay the same. Old habits are demolished. Inferior ways of thinking are ripped out. Dark places are exposed. No room is safe. Sometimes things look messier as a result. But before God is done, He replaces panic with faith, hate with love, complaint with prayer, and selfishness with generosity. Everything changes.

WHEN THE SPIRIT OF GOD MOVES IN, A MASSIVE RENOVATION TAKES PLACE! WE CANNOT STAY THE SAME.

James is here to help swing the hammer. He's going to bang on some old walls. Some of what he says will hurt! But if we deeply take in what he is saying, we will discover the joy of integrity—having the outside of our lives match the inside, our conduct matching our confession. The world needs to see the beauty of the gospel displayed in the activity of God's people. James will help us get there.

Leading a group? Download the leader guide at *threadsmedia.com/thischangeseverything.*

IDENTITY
SHIFT

FIRE CHIEF

We had two patrols when I was in elementary school. The first was the safety patrol, which directed traffic while students exited the school. (I'm not convinced putting fifth graders in charge of traffic was a good idea.) The second was the fire patrol, which timed the evacuation drills and reported their findings to the school over the intercom (a *huge* deal when you're 10 years old). Through a little help from my brother and his friends, I was elected chief of the fire patrol at my elementary school. That meant that if a fire drill was conducted, I had certain responsibilities to ensure the safety of other students.

About a month into my fifth-grade year, the alarm went off. I was sitting in math class and our teacher said, "Students, get in line and walk toward the back of the school." I was a student, so I got in line and began to file out like everybody else. Until about midway down the hall it hit me: *Wait a minute; I'm the fire chief. I shouldn't be going this way. The stopwatch is in the desk in the assistant principal's office at the front of the school!* In that moment, panic struck my little heart: *What should I do? If I get out of line I'll look weird, and what will everyone think?* After a few seconds (which felt like an eternity) the crisis was resolved for me when I remembered the day that the principal of our school appointed me fire chief. The highest authority in the school had given me a new identity, and that held more weight than the title of "student."

I stepped out of line.

As little eyes around me widened in terror, I began to run the opposite direction. Feeling the stares of my entire class, I sprinted, yelling, "I am the fire chief!"

Why mention this? Because James will call for a revolution in lifestyle. He will do it forcefully! What kind of guy calls you "brothers" and "adulteresses" in the same letter? I will tell you: someone unafraid to shoot straight with you. The Book of James packs more commands per square inch than any other book in the Bible. He demands a changed life. Yet it's critical to understand that James does not call us to alter our behavior in order to earn God's approval. Rather, because we have had a radical alteration of *identity*, this leads to a natural alteration of *activity*.

God has no interest in trying to make normal people drink less or cuss less or go to church more. God does not aim at adding a little more religion to our lives. God designs to change us on the inside—a total renovation of our identity. When this occurs, then a natural change in activity takes place.

James will speak this way because this is exactly what happened to him. He did not always believe that Jesus was the Lord.

JAMES, THE SKEPTIC

Before we go any further, we need to gather some background on James. Let's look at the Gospel of Matthew and the early explosion of Jesus' ministry.

> "And coming to his hometown he taught them in their synagogue, so that they were astonished, and said, 'Where did this man get this wisdom and these mighty works? Is not this the carpenter's son? Is not his mother called Mary? And are not his brothers James and Joseph and Simon and Judas?'" (Matthew 13:54-55).

Based on this passage, who was James?

One of the first times James, the author of the Book of James and the brother of Jesus, shows up in the Bible is in Mark 3 during Jesus' early ministry. Jesus proclaimed Himself as the healer of the sick, the forgiver of sins, and the groom sent to love God's people, the bride, forever. Powerful stuff. The healings in particular drew quite a following. Into that moment of intense popularity, His family arrives. What will the siblings of this new prophet say to the crowd? Will they confirm His station as the One sent from God? Will they bow at His feet in worship? Will they stand at His side as the cabinet of His new administration?

"Then he went home, and the crowd gathered again, so that they could not even eat. And when his family heard it, they went out to seize him, for they were saying, 'He is out of his mind'" (Mark 3:20-21).

How did Jesus' family, which included His brother James, respond to His ministry?

What impact do you think this might have had on their family relationships?

Just when Jesus' public ministry began gaining some momentum, James and Jesus' other brothers came to take custody of Him because they thought He was insane. Not only did Jesus' family think He had lost His mind, they were saying it to people in the crowd—not necessarily a glowing endorsement of His campaign.

The next time we encounter James is in John 7, later in Jesus' ministry.

"After this Jesus went about in Galilee. He would not go about in Judea, because the Jews were seeking to kill him. Now the Jews' Feast of Booths was at hand. So his brothers said to him, 'Leave here and go to Judea, that your disciples also may see the works you are doing. For no one works in secret if he seeks to be known openly. If you do these things, show yourself to the world.' For not even his brothers believed in him" (John 7:1-5).

What do these verses tell us about Jesus' brothers?

Why did they encourage Jesus to show Himself to the world?

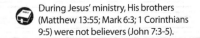
During Jesus' ministry, His brothers (Matthew 13:55; Mark 6:3; 1 Corinthians 9:5) were not believers (John 7:3-5).

In Mark 3 they were trying to pull Jesus away from the crowds, and now they are encouraging Him to go to the most crowded event in the region and promote Himself. What is happening here? John tells us their motivation:

"For not even his brothers believed in him" (John 7:5).

Their goading Him to appear in Jerusalem was not a vote of support. They were being sarcastic. Their disbelief in their brother had hardened into disdain and mockery.

A RADICAL CHANGE

After the Gospels, the next time we encounter James in the Bible he was leading the fledgling church in the Book of Acts. In Galatians 2:9 the apostle Paul called him a "pillar" of the church. In Acts 12:16-17, when the apostle Peter was miraculously released from prison, he immediately told his friends to go and tell James. In Acts 15, when the early church debated the particulars of the nature of salvation, James led the counsel that decisively outlined the nature of faith and works!

The last time we encounter James is in the writings of the ancient historians Josephus and Eusebius. The Jewish religious leadership in Jerusalem demanded that James publicly denounce claims that Jesus was the Messiah. James not only refused, but he also boldly declared that his brother "is sitting in heaven at the right hand of the great power, and he will come on the clouds of heaven."[1] They responded by stoning him to death. James willingly died proclaiming that his brother was God's chosen instrument to rescue humanity from our sin.

Here in his letter, look at how James introduced himself:

"James, a servant of God and of the Lord Jesus Christ, To the twelve tribes in the Dispersion: Greetings" (v. 1).

How does that happen? How did James move from mocking Jesus to leading the Jesus movement? From doubting Jesus' sanity to boldly dying for Jesus? How did he go from skeptic about Jesus to servant of Jesus?

 Examine how other apostles introduced themselves by reading Romans 1:1-7; 1 Peter 1:1-2; and 2 John 1:1-3.

What do you think caused this shift?

James had a radical change in identity. He saw himself completely differently, and it is entirely the result of a shift in His perspective on Jesus. What happened here? We need to understand this because this transformation is exactly what God wants for us. This radical alteration of identity is what James will assume happened to each of us before he issues a single command about how we were meant to live. We need to get our minds around this.

Write down the names of some people you think would *never* become sold-out followers of Jesus. Try to imagine: What do you think it would take for them to change?

JAMES, A SERVANT OF GOD
Going back to James's description of himself, let's break down each part individually.

The first identifier, "servant of God," while significant, was not entirely revolutionary. You can find this title applied to great leaders of the people of God all throughout the Old Testament (Moses in Deuteronomy 34:5; Daniel 9:11 and David in Jeremiah 33:21; Ezekiel 37:25).

The revolutionary title is the next one—*servant of the Lord Jesus Christ;* this marks a shift. James was not just a servant of God, but a servant or slave of a person.

For some of us, familiarity with these terms prevents us from grasping the significance of what the man just said. Permit me to supply a few definitions to help us appreciate the gravity of this declaration. First, the term *servant* obviously carries the idea of service. However, it also indicates ownership. In the first century, servants (or slaves) worked for those who owned them.

So calling oneself "owned and in the service of" God can sound impressive. Calling oneself "owned and in the service of" another person does not sound impressive at all. That is a lowly title.

What's your instinctual reaction to a title like this?

What do you think would prompt James to adopt an identifier like this and wear it so comfortably?

While the lowliness of his self-identifier may shock some, it pales in comparison to the audacity of the descriptors he bestows on his master. James flanks the name "Jesus" with two important titles: *Lord* and *Christ*.

The term *Christ* means "anointed one." Anointing meant that one had been designated for a particular task. Kings were anointed to serve as rulers. Priests were anointed to serve God. As God revealed His plans to humanity, more and more the idea emerged that God had selected someone to serve as a Ruler of humanity and as a Servant of God. James identifies Jesus as the capital "C" Christ, one anointed by God for His special purposes. Yet he does not stop there. The term *Lord* carries even greater significance.

Lord can mean "master." Yet it went far beyond that for the early church. The Septuagint, the Greek translation of the Old Testament, translated the name *Yahweh,* the personal name for God, as *Lord*. So, for the Christian, this word carried the idea of deity.

In the Roman world of James's day, the ruler of Rome demanded to be worshiped as god. All living under the power of the Roman Empire were expected to offer a pinch of incense and proclaim, "Caesar is Lord." The Christians would not do this because Caesar was not Lord. Only Jesus was Lord. This was one of the main reasons for persecution in the early church. Christians were killed not for worshiping Jesus but for worshiping *only* Jesus!

So we need to grab the shocking significance of James's introduction. He says: (1) I am a slave of God and (2) I am a slave of that man, Jesus, who is God!

James had a radical change of identity from skeptic of Jesus to servant of Jesus. What do you think caused this change?

A RADICAL CONFRONTATION

I left out one important mention of James in the New Testament. He appears in 1 Corinthians 15.

> "For I delivered to you as of first importance what I also received: that Christ died for our sins in accordance with the Scriptures, that he was buried, that he was raised on the third day in accordance with the Scriptures, and that he appeared to Cephas, then to the twelve. Then he appeared to more than five hundred brothers at one time, most of whom are still alive, though some have fallen asleep. Then he appeared to James, then to all the apostles" (vv. 3-7).

What happened to James? What impact do you think this had?

What impact would it have had on you?

 After the resurrection and ascension, the brothers of Jesus were said to have been with the Twelve and the other believers in Jerusalem (Acts 1:14).

James went from mockery to leading this movement that has impacted the globe and writing a book that has influenced humanity for generations. How did this transition from skeptic to servant occur? One simple answer: James had a personal encounter with the risen Jesus. This is the pivot point. Before this moment, James was skeptical, if not hostile, toward the idea that Jesus was and is the Messiah. After this moment, James not only supported his brother, but gave his very life to proclaim to the world that Jesus is the Son of God come to save us.

The resurrection of Jesus can change you and your most skeptical friends as well. Two aspects of this historic event confronted James. The first is the *reality* that Jesus died and rose. The second is the *reason* that Jesus died and rose. Let's take them one at a time.

THE REALITY THAT HE DIED AND ROSE

The change in James's life came as a response to an objective reality he had to face and come to terms with: the reality of the space-time event of the death and resurrection of Jesus Christ. The resurrection changed James's mind on the nature and authority of Jesus. It is a reality that we must deal with as well. Paul laid it out in 1 Corinthians 15.

Go back and read 1 Corinthians 15:3-7 again. What two things make a strong case that the resurrection of Jesus was an actual historical event?

Paul presented this evidence as of "first importance." Notice it is an argument, a presentation of historical evidence to prove to you that Jesus is who He said He is. First, he points out that Jesus was buried and then rose. There is an empty tomb. Second, he maintains that Jesus was seen by many eyewitnesses, people whom James identifies as still alive in his day. Why mention this? Presumably

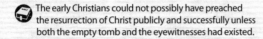 The early Christians could not possibly have preached the resurrection of Christ publicly and successfully unless both the empty tomb and the eyewitnesses had existed.

THIS CHANGES EVERYTHING

it's because they were alive and willing to discuss the resurrection of Jesus! The early church grew rapidly because men and women fanned out across the world spreading the message of the man who died and rose.

Together these pieces of evidence—the empty tomb and the bold, confessing eyewitnesses—provide compelling evidence for the historicity of the resurrection of Jesus. The historian N.T. Wright said it this way:

> "Neither the empty tomb by itself, however, nor the appearances by themselves, could have generated the early Christian belief. The empty tomb alone would be a puzzle and a tragedy. Sightings of an apparently alive Jesus, by themselves, would have been classified as visions or hallucinations, which were well enough known in the ancient world.... However, an empty tomb and appearances of a living Jesus, taken together, would have presented a powerful reason for the emergence of the belief."[2]

The amount of detail given in the Gospels reads like eyewitness accounts. It shows that they cannot be fiction, and therefore what James experienced is true—Jesus is the Risen Savior.

How has Jesus' resurrection impacted your life—both theologically and practically?

When we come to the conclusion that Jesus actually rose from the dead, we have no choice but to proclaim Him as God—and then bow down and worship Him as He deserves.

I want you to have a confrontation with the risen Christ.

 When other historical messianic figures died, their followers reacted as the disciples on the Emmaus Road did after the crucifixion: "We had hoped that he was the one to redeem Israel," but they were wrong (Luke 24:21). One does not logically infer resurrection from crucifixion, and it only happened in the case of Christ.

By this I don't mean I want you to have a complicated, emotional experience. That was not the basis of James's transformation. We are not confronted by a feeling that Jesus has power over life and death; we are confronted by the reality that He does. This is not a call to interact with the mystical but with the historical. I challenge you to face the facts. No one changed history like this man, and He believed He was God. We must deal with this incredible claim: Jesus claimed to be God and then beat death.

When James realized who his brother was, it changed everything about him. James not only moved from skeptic to believer; he moved from skeptic to servant! If this man really is God, then what Scripture says about Him being the Maker of the world is true. That means He owns me, and my life is His. This is the first transformative fact of the resurrection: It shows us that Jesus has power over our lives. We must submit to Him as Lord.

If we're honest, *must submit* doesn't sound like a lot of fun. Who wants to be a servant? How can this be good news? This is the second aspect of the resurrection that changed James: not just the *reality* that Jesus died and rose, but the *reason* why He did it. When we see the *reality*, we stand in awe of His power. When we see the *reason*, we stand in wonder at His love.

THE REASON THAT HE DIED AND ROSE

Several years ago I was invited to speak at a camp that hosted several churches from around the country. I arrived early and spent some time visiting with the staff of the camp. As we chatted, a truck loaded with luggage pulled up alongside us. An exasperated looking youth pastor began to bark orders at me: "Why are you standing there? Get these bags and take them into my cabin." I said, "OK," and I loaded his bags into his cabin. A few minutes later the director of the camp showed up. As I finished unloading, the director looked at the youth pastor and said, "Oh, I see you've met our camp pastor for the week." The youth pastor looked at me horrified. He had treated me like an errand-boy (which, by the way, he still should've treated with respect), when I was actually there to guide the camp spiritually. I will never forget the look on his face. He apologized somewhere around 40 times before the camp was over.

 All of the Gospels indicate that the initial report of the empty tomb came from women. This is unusual for the culture and shows that this detail was not one constructed by the church. A woman's testimony would not have been respected in the culture.

Now if that was embarrassing for this pastor, imagine how James must have felt when he encountered the risen Jesus. At the same moment it dawned on James that this man must be God, the thought had to cross his mind, *I've been treating Him like He was nuts for years! I made fun of Him!* How awkward must that initial meeting have been? Do you think Jesus gave James a hard time? "C'mon bro, virgin birth! You could have figured it out!" What do you think that interaction was like? I'll tell you one thing we do know: It was revolutionary because James emerged changed forever.

This raises an important question: Why don't we meet an apologetic, embarrassed James in this epistle? Why was he not condemned forever to be mocked as the man who failed to realize God was living in the same house with him for decades? I'll tell you why. Knowing the objective fact that Jesus actually lived, died, and rose from the dead will give you a holy fear of Him. Knowing *why* He did it will give you a heart for Him.

> **"For I delivered to you as of first importance what I also received: that Christ died for our sins in accordance with the Scriptures"** (1 Corinthians 15:3).

What does "Christ died for our sins" mean to you?

Jesus died for our sins. Sin literally means "missing the mark." There was something we were meant to be, and we aren't yet it. The Bible says without God we're incomplete, not yet finished, not who we should be. And we all feel this; we know we should be different than we are. We try to fix ourselves, but we can't. When we realize that God had to die to take away our sin, it humbles us. When we realize that God willingly chose to die to forgive our sins, it raises us up. When we realize that the guy who runs the show loves us, that's when we know we're going to be OK. Jesus did not return from the grave to rub James's sins in his face. He rose from the grave to forgive James's sins and cast them away forever!

Nobody thinks they are living up to what they should be—nobody. Yet through the resurrection, God stamped "paid in full" across all of our sin. And here's the incredible part: When we believe in Christ, we are no longer seen by our record, but by Jesus' perfect record. He makes us clean. When we grasp this, we don't simply honor Jesus for His power, but we joyfully give ourselves to Him because we're in awe of His great love.

Do you currently feel a struggle within you to meet standards that you are constantly falling short of? Explain your response.

Is your identity often based on your performance? How so?

Look back to what you wrote as your descriptor/identifier on page 14 of this chapter. What clues does this give you as to where you truly find your identity?

What would it look like for you to live in the identity of a servant of God and Jesus? What does that mean on a daily basis?

+ Church tradition notes the exceptional piety of James, reporting that his knees were like those of a camel due to the unusual amounts of time he spent in prayer.[3]

THIS CHANGES EVERYTHING

Years ago I remember hearing a pastor tell the story of a husband and wife picnicking in the park. Suddenly they found themselves in the midst of a violent hailstorm. Softball-sized chunks of ice hurled from the sky. They tried to hide, but they were in a field where no shelter could be found. So the husband did the only thing he could do: He held his wife's body close so his body would shield her from the onslaught. The wife recalled later that she could feel his body shake under the concussive force of the hailstones as they struck his body again and again. Finally, one struck his head. Before he lost consciousness, his final act was to fall on top of his wife, so his unconscious body could continue to protect her.

Then I remember the pastor looking out at us and asking the question, "Now, when that woman stood at the foot of her husband's hospital bed, what thoughts do you think filled her mind as she saw his scars, knowing that they came from this supreme act of love for her?" Then he answered his own question: "I think every scar would be an emblem of love to her. I believe she would rejoice that she belonged to a man who would willingly give himself up for her like that."

It is the same for the Christian. It's easy to give away your life to a man who gave His life for you. Belonging to Him is not a burden; it is a delight.

MOVING FORWARD

The Letter of James is going to call for life-change. Yet you've got to be a servant of God before learning *how* to serve Him means anything. So before you start making a checklist of how you'll change all manner of activities in your life, stop and ponder the One who can change your identity. He makes sinners into saints. He turns the lost into the found. He makes the broken whole, the dead alive, and the skeptic a joyful servant. And He can change you.

I challenge you to investigate the Person of Jesus as we make our way through the Epistle of James. Concentrate on the reality that Jesus lived, died, and rose again. When you feel convicted or shamed because of your sin, remind yourself that Jesus came to take away your shame and to give you new life—to make you a child of God.

If you can grab those realities, you won't be the same person anymore. You'll be able to say joyfully with James that you are a servant of the Lord Jesus Christ. Fix your eyes on Jesus. Because when you truly see Him, it changes everything.

APPLY TO LIFE

> **REFLECT:** What do you hope to learn about yourself as you study the Epistle of James?

> **CONNECT:** People have a wide range of opinions about who Jesus is and what His purpose on earth was. Part of our job as Christians is to inform people of the truth of Jesus' identity and work—the gospel. Christ established the church and uses it to reach the world with the truth of His life, death, and resurrection. The church plays a vital role in God's plan for the world, and, likewise, ought to play a vital role in our lives. Brainstorm with members of your church how you can work together to share the truth of the gospel of Christ.

> **LISTEN:** Purchase "The Death of Death" by Charlie Hall and "The Gospel Changes Everything" by Meredith Andrews from the *This Changes Everything* playlist. Add these to your regular mix of music throughout the week to continue thinking about your identity in Christ.

NOTES

JOY IN PAIN

THIS CHANGES EVERYTHING

"Count it all joy, my brothers, when you meet trials of various kinds, for you know that the testing of your faith produces steadfastness. And let steadfastness have its full effect, that you may be perfect and complete, lacking in nothing. If any of you lacks wisdom, let him ask God, who gives generously to all without reproach, and it will be given him. But let him ask in faith, with no doubting, for the one who doubts is like a wave of the sea that is driven and tossed by the wind. For that person must not suppose that he will receive anything from the Lord; he is a double-minded man, unstable in all his ways. Let the lowly brother boast in his exaltation, and the rich in his humiliation, because like a flower of the grass he will pass away. For the sun rises with its scorching heat and withers the grass; its flower falls, and its beauty perishes. So also will the rich man fade away in the midst of his pursuits. Blessed is the man who remains steadfast under trial, for when he has stood the test he will receive the crown of life, which God has promised to those who love him."

James 1:2-12

Read James 1:2-12. What stands out to you?

What's your first reaction to the command to rejoice in trials?

Hannah, my 1-year-old baby girl, thrills my heart. She possesses boundless curiosity. I love watching this little person I cherish experience one "first" after another: touching sand, watching a light switch turn on, eating her first strawberry. I delight in introducing her to the beauty and wonder of the world.

A few weeks into Hannah's life, the time came to take her to get vaccines. Disease runs rampant in our world, and if we fail to prepare her little body, then any number of viruses could claim her life. So I carried my little girl into a cold, sterile office and held her down as nurses stuck needles into her little legs. I will never forget the look in her eyes. It was as if she were screaming, "Betrayal! Why would you put me through this?" I remember thinking in that moment, *Here's another first. My daughter is learning that this world is filled with pain.*

REJOICE WHEN (NOT IF) YOU FACE TRIALS
James wrote to Christians, the children of God who have been brought forth by the Word of their Father in heaven. In the second verse, James lays out his first lesson on trials.

"Count it all joy, my brothers, when you meet trials of various kinds."

There's a lot happening in this verse, but I want you to notice first that he said, "*whenever* you face trials" (NIV). Lesson 1: Trials are inevitable. James wants us to know that suffering is part of this world, and Christians are not exempt. Jesus warned His disciples, "You will have suffering in this world" (John 16:33, HCSB). Paul told his followers, "Through many tribulations we must enter the kingdom of God" (Acts 14:22). Those who think that Christians should not have to suffer simply have not read the Bible. The entire New Testament shouts to us that trials are coming. Peter told his people, "Do not be surprised at the fiery trial when it comes upon you to test you, as though something strange were happening to you" (1 Peter 4:12). We should not be shocked by trials when they come. We should expect difficulty in this life.

If you look back at our text, James takes it a step further than Peter. James calls us not only to expect difficulties, but to rejoice in the midst of them!

If that sounds strange, let me assure you, it is. It gets weirder, because James is not done. Notice he does not say, "Rejoice when *a* trial comes—when your latté is too cold, when you do not get the job you want, or when your girlfriend breaks up with you." He says, "Consider it pure joy, my brothers, whenever you face trials" (NIV). On top of that, the word *face* means "to fall into the midst of" something. So James calls us to rejoice when we slip, stumble, and find ourselves surrounded by a multitude of trials.

Watch the *This Changes Everything* video for Session 2, available at *threadsmedia.com/thischangeseverything*.

THIS CHANGES EVERYTHING

In other words, James says you should rejoice when your latté is too cold while you're on the way to a job you did not want, and your girl breaks up with you on the way . . . and then you get hit by a car. In that moment, as you lay there broken and bleeding, James calls you to celebrate!

Now, to be serious, the reality stands that many of us are presently facing trials of various kinds. They range from frustrating commutes to strained relationships. From a nagging cold to a debilitating illness. Pain is the one experience common to all of humanity. Not everyone gets happiness, but everyone gets pain. Here James unflinchingly stares at our harshest realities and commands us to count them all joy.

What trials are you currently experiencing?

Now at this point I imagine that some skeptics among us are ready to write off James. Seriously, who rejoices in trials? Either someone who is totally fake and pretends everything is wonderful when it is not, or someone who has totally lost touch with reality and thinks smoking is good for you, Twinkies® are a low-calorie snack, and pain is fun.

Before you become too skeptical, understand that there's another group of people who can rejoice even in the midst of pain. They are the people who know something. There's something going on within the trial and pain they're experiencing that makes them joyful.

REJOICE BECAUSE YOU KNOW SOMETHING

Take, for example, a weight lifter. What happens when you lift weights? You put your muscles in crisis. You put them through a trial. You put them in pain! You do it because you are confident that putting those muscles through suffering results in muscle growth. You are so sure that this current crisis will result in a desirable outcome (good health, a ripped set of abs) that you feel happy, even while you're still in the midst of the pain of the workout! That's why you hear dudes in the gym say things like, "Oh man, that burn is good." No it's not; the burn hurts! Yet you're so sure it will produce a desired outcome that joy comes flooding into your soul even while you are in the midst of the physical pain.

Do you see it? Knowing that *something* good can come from trials brings us joy even in the midst of the pain.

So is James calling us to be out of touch with reality? Or is he calling us to be people who know something wonderful that brings joy even in the midst of trials? Look at verse 3.

"For you know that the testing of your faith produces steadfastness."

We know something! We can be joyful in the midst of trials because we know that the tests we endure have potential locked up in them. They can produce something positive. Namely, they can forge in us "steadfastness" or "perseverance" (NIV). The original Greek word is *hupomone*, which is actually a combination of two smaller words. *Mone* means "to abide or flourish" and *hupo* means "under." So the idea behind this "steadfastness" is that you can abide under a great deal of stress—and not just exist under it, but thrive and flourish even under something difficult and heavy. James tells us that, much like a weight lifter, we can find joy in the midst of crisis because we know that it can make us stronger people.

In his book *Crazy for the Storm,* Norman Ollestad tells the story of an 11-year-old boy who overcame incredible odds to survive a plane crash on top of a mountain in the midst of a blizzard. Throughout the book the boy, now an adult, flashes back to moments in his childhood with his father.

During his young life his father would purposefully put him in challenging situations. They went skiing, and his dad would take him to progressively harder slopes. They went surfing, and his father would lead him out to larger and larger waves. Page after page he relates stories of moments when his father would place him in situations that tested the limits of his capacities. Yet in those moments his father would teach him the tools and techniques he needed to ski down the hill or surf the big wave. Over time, situations that used to be difficult for the boy were no longer scary. It even became fun. Fast-forward to this horrible accident. There in the midst of these extreme conditions, the boy realizes that he has the ability to survive in these harsh circumstances because his father had placed him in so many trials throughout his youth. Trials had forged in him endurance—the ability to flourish under great amounts of strain.[1]

When have you endured a trial that made you a stronger person?

How could the trials you are enduring now help you develop as a person?

According to James, we gain steadfastness, or endurance, when we go through the inevitable trials of life. And that's a good thing. It is a helpful thing. But it is not enough.

THE GAIN FROM PAIN: WISDOM

The first few times I preached on these verses in James, I stopped at this point right here. I told the crowd, "When we go through trials, God blesses us by building up our endurance." And then I would give a bunch of examples and send everybody home.

Recently I've realized that it is insufficient to say, "We should endure pain because it will give us the ability to endure more pain." In other words, "Take a beating because doing so will allow us to take a harder beating next time." That doesn't seem like enough information to produce lasting joy. We need more.

Thankfully, that's not where James stops.

"And let steadfastness have its full effect, that you may be perfect and complete, lacking in nothing" (v. 4).

According to James, what other benefits come as a result of enduring trials?

James points out that enduring difficult circumstances can not only give us the ability to withstand greater trials, but it can both furnish us with character qualities we lack and improve the admirable qualities we already possess! We see this all the time. Think of any of the "hero stories" you enjoy in literature or movies. The main character faces a daunting trial. As he moves through the crisis, he doesn't simply endure hardship; he faces the challenge in a way that gives him new resources with which to overcome difficulties and unlocks potential that has been buried deep within.

Step out of the world of fiction and the principle holds true. Think of the people you admire. It is typically those people who not only endured great suffering, but went through it in such a way that it made them better people. Trials carry the potential not only to build up our endurance but to fill out our character.

Name people you admire. How did suffering make them the impressive person they are today?

Now before we discover how exactly trials build character, we must notice that there's something we must do. James said we must "*Let steadfastness* have its full effect" (emphasis mine). We have to allow trials to teach us. Let me be clear: We are not guaranteed growth by going through trials. We can suffer and not learn a thing. We can go through hardship and it make us bitter, not better. The question we have to ask ourselves is, *Am I humble enough to accept pain as a teacher?* I hope so, because the benefits are substantial.

How does our culture teach us to respond to trials and suffering?

How do you naturally react to difficult circumstances and personal pain? Why?

What does suffering give us? We find it in the verbal connection of verses 4-5.

> **"And let steadfastness have its full effect, that you may be perfect and complete, lacking in nothing"** (v. 4).

> **"If any of you lacks wisdom, let him ask God, who gives generously to all without reproach, and it will be given him"** (v. 5).

Do you see it? Trials fill us up with the things we lack. What do we lack? Wisdom!

What is wisdom? Simply stated: Wisdom is an understanding of how the world works and the ability to navigate it well. Wise people have a firm grasp of reality and know how to flourish in it. And here's the hard truth: Wisdom is not something we are born with.

Just like earthly parents use difficult circumstances to teach their kids, God, in His wisdom, will often use pain to make us wise. He will put you in situations where you feel overwhelmed and suddenly you have to learn a whole different way to respond. Not all wisdom needs to be gained through pain, but pain is an excellent teacher.

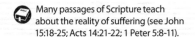 Many passages of Scripture teach about the reality of suffering (see John 15:18-25; Acts 14:21-22; 1 Peter 5:8-11).

What images or ideas come to mind when you hear the word *wisdom*? Why?

List some people you consider wise. What makes them wise in your eyes?

This is the big reveal. This is why we can rejoice in the midst of suffering—because we know that suffering can make us wiser. Every trial we face holds the power to transform us into people who see the world clearly and respond to circumstances appropriately. If we will allow it, trials can bring us great wisdom. Now, only one question remains: How exactly do trials give us wisdom?

THE BENEFITS OF WISDOM

Let's get specific. I've said that wisdom will help us know how the world works and how to navigate through it, but what does that mean exactly? James identified two insights that we can learn from trials.[2]

1. Trials can give us the wisdom to release our grip on things that fade.
Read James 1:9-11:

> "Let the lowly brother boast in his exaltation, and the rich in his humiliation, because like a flower of the grass he will pass away. For the sun rises with its scorching heat and withers the grass; its flower falls, and its beauty perishes. So also will the rich man fade away in the midst of his pursuits."

What do you find most interesting about these verses? Why?

James encourages the poor not to be too distraught by their lack of funds, because money will ultimately fade. Likewise, he warns the rich not to put their hope in their finances.

If we're not careful, we can care too much about things that do not last. We can look to temporal things such as money, beauty, popularity, titles, or prestige to give us a sense of comfort and self-worth. That's a terrible mistake, because these things will not last.

Some of us learned this lesson in high school. We built our entire sense of identity on our status, friendship groups, and our accomplishments. Then we stood upon the mountaintop of our successes, wearing our letter jackets, and declared to the world, "I have arrived!" But then we went to college or started our first job in that same letter jacket, and nobody cared about our previous accomplishments. There is nothing wrong with enjoying your high school years. But if you have been in a perpetual funk since graduation, then you did more than enjoy high school; you made it your source of worth.

If we're not careful, we will make our beauty, our money, or our success the source of life, and that's a terrible mistake. It is a bad investment. And sometimes God, in His mercy, will bring pain to snap us out of wasting our lives doing this.

Breaking my femur in high school was one of the best things that ever happened to me (though I certainly didn't think so at the time). Up to that point, success in football, and the approval that it would bring me, was much more important to me than God (though I would have never said that out loud). God used pain to sync me back up with reality, and I thank Him for it.

 Proverbs 3:19 says, "The LORD by wisdom founded the earth; by understanding he established the heavens." Proverbs 28:26 says, "Whoever trusts in his own mind is a fool, but he who walks in wisdom will be delivered."

Which element of your life (your beautiful hair, huge muscles, job, car, home, bank account, or the approval of someone) would bring devastation to you if you lost it?

Has God ever taken something from you, or deprived you of something you wanted, and later you were grateful that He did? Explain.

2. Trials can give us the wisdom to focus on what will last forever and to look toward God.

When we experience pain it can snap us out of putting too much hope in things that will not last. At the same time, it can cause us to look beyond our current circumstances and realize that there is more to life than what we experience here.

Read verse 12:

> "Blessed is the man who remains steadfast under trial, for when he has stood the test he will receive the crown of life, which God has promised to those who love him."

Pain will make us look up to pay attention to God. It helps us see what has always been true: that we desperately need Him.

In his book *Beautiful Boy*, David Sheff gives a candid account of his struggle as a father watching his son, his "beautiful boy," spiral down into the dark pit of meth addiction. At one point a drug and alcohol counselor says to him: "God bless you . . . he's in God's hands." Sheff records his response: "It startles me. I mention that our family never believed in God." The counselor answers, "You will believe in God before this is over."[3] After numerous trips in and out of rehab, his son finally gets clean. He meets a girl, lands a great job, even gets a book deal. Then he relapses. In a heart-wrenching chapter, Sheff faces the brutal truth:

+ Wisdom teaches us that pain is a part of this life and yet there is something bigger than pain that guides all things to produce glorious purposes.

THIS CHANGES EVERYTHING

"Despite my knowledge that addiction does not respond to logic, I have held on to a vestige of the idea that the trappings of a life—girlfriend, job, money, solid friendships, a desire to do right by those you love—can make it OK, but they don't."[4]

With every earthly incentive and threat spent, this broken man begins to repeat the phrase over and over again, "Please God heal Nic." And God did. By the end of the book, the author does not wish this terrible ordeal on anyone. He finds himself experiencing a sense of gratitude for the lessons this pain has taught him.

This is the great gift that trials can give. They teach us to release our insane grip on that which will not last, and they beckon us to grip onto the One who endures forever. As we look up, we realize that there will be an end to this trouble. God has made glorious promises to us, and we can cling to them in times of trouble. All of this pain will end and a glorious future awaits those who trust in Him.

"For this light momentary affliction is preparing for us an eternal weight of glory beyond all comparison, as we look not to the things that are seen but to the things that are unseen. For the things that are seen are transient, but the things that are unseen are eternal" (2 Corinthians 4:17-18).

"But recall the former days when, after you were enlightened, you endured a hard struggle with sufferings, sometimes being publicly exposed to reproach and affliction, and sometimes being partners with those so treated. For you had compassion on those in prison, and you joyfully accepted the plundering of your property, since you knew that you yourselves had a better possession and an abiding one. Therefore do not throw away your confidence, which has a great reward. For you have need of endurance, so that when you have done the will of God you may receive what is promised" (Hebrews 10:32-36).

There is life beyond our pain. Our suffering is real, but it is temporary.

"We can rest contentedly in our sins . . . we can ignore even pleasure. But pain insists upon being attended to. God whispers to us in our pleasures, speaks in our conscience, but shouts in our pains: it is His megaphone to rouse a deaf world." —C.S. Lewis[5]

Does understanding that pain is temporary impact the affect it has on you? Explain.

James wrote that the man who remains steadfast under trial "will receive the crown of life, which God has promised to those who love him" (1:12). The reason we can rejoice in the midst of suffering is because it gives us a chance to recognize that something out there—Someone out there—is bigger than our suffering. Even better, it helps us remember that Someone has already done something about our suffering.

How does this knowledge affect your view of suffering?

Wisdom allows us to step back and look at the big-picture story of our lives—to see there is a wonderful God in control, and that He made us beautiful. He made this world good and pristine and glorious. But sin came into play, a breaking with God, and everything got damaged. The world is not how it should be, which means we are right to rage against the darkness and the pain.

Wisdom allows us to remember that our God is so wonderful He wouldn't leave us in pain. He entered this world, coming to us as Jesus Christ. He walked among us, and in His love, He's generous even to the most sin-sick and degenerated of people.

Remember John 1:

> **"And the Word became flesh and dwelt among us, and we have**
> **seen his glory, glory as of the only Son from the Father, full of**
> **grace and truth . . . from his fullness we have all received, grace**
> **upon grace" (vv. 14,16).**

Wisdom allows us to see God's wisdom and how it confounds the sages of the day and confounds us still. We can see His justice, His sense of truth and rightness—that He'll declare what's right and yet still manage to do so graciously.

And once again we begin to see our trials as something in which we can rejoice—not because we know all the reasons why we are enduring them, but because we know Jesus. We know He can take even our pain and make it glorious if we trust Him.

Let me close with a story. Not long after I became director of Breakaway Ministries, I learned that one of our sweet volunteers, a beautiful young woman, had been diagnosed with stage IV metastatic melanoma, the deadliest form of skin cancer. It originated in a mole on her left shoulder blade. The cancer worked its way into her lymph nodes, and tumors began to appear in her brain, lungs, and abdomen. She lost all her hair, but none of her beauty. She radiated with a joy unspeakable, even in the midst of tremendous pain. She died the week I taught this text at Breakaway. Mutual friends of ours directed me to her online journal, where I read a powerful post entitled "Sovereign, Sanctifying Scars." I will close with her words:

> JULY 28—SOVEREIGN, SANCTIFYING SCARS
> " . . . I recently read a quote from Joni Eareckson in my Bible study
> that said: 'If I could, I would take this wheelchair to heaven with
> me. Standing next to my Savior, Jesus Christ, I would say, "Lord,
> do you see this wheelchair? Well, before you send it to hell, I want
> to tell you something about it. You were right when you said that
> in this world we would have trouble. There's a lot of trouble being
> a quadriplegic. But you know what? The weaker I was in that

thing the harder I leaned on you, and the harder I leaned on you, the stronger I discovered you to be. Thank you for the bruising blessing it was, this severe mercy. Thank you.'"

"Wow! What if we all began to view our suffering, be it physical, emotional, relational—as a Bruising Blessing, a Severe Mercy—our scars, wheelchairs, bald heads . . . all reminding us of God's sovereignty?!?! Yes, when we live our lives in complete submission to our Creator we can look at each and every scar as a Sovereign, Sanctifying Scar. A scar that, because of God's complete sovereignty and His ability and desire to rid us of our sin, helps to lead us into the enjoyment of having a right relationship with God. Therein lies the true blessing of being bruised. Each blessing is found amidst the deep, indescribable relationship that develops between you and God as you trust in Him. Lean on Him and He will turn your 'Valley of Baca' into a place of springs!"[6]

APPLY TO LIFE

> **CONNECT:** As you go through this week, pay attention to the trials you face. Journal about these—big and small—to see what God is revealing to you.

> **STUDY:** Read Revelation 21:3-7. How do you respond to these verses? What encouragement do you find for the trials you are facing?

> **LISTEN:** Purchase "Joy" by BridgeCity and "Raise My Voice" by Robbie Seay Band from the *This Changes Everything* playlist. Add these to your regular mix of music throughout the week to remind you to remain joyful in the midst of suffering.

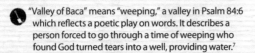 "Valley of Baca" means "weeping," a valley in Psalm 84:6 which reflects a poetic play on words. It describes a person forced to go through a time of weeping who found God turned tears into a well, providing water.[7]

THIS CHANGES EVERYTHING

Psalm 30:5

NOTES

WITH EVERY TRIAL A TEMPTATION

> "Let no one say when he is tempted, 'I am being tempted by God,' for God cannot be tempted with evil, and he himself tempts no one. But each person is tempted when he is lured and enticed by his own desire. Then desire when it has conceived gives birth to sin, and sin when it is fully grown brings forth death. Do not be deceived, my beloved brothers."

James 1:13-16

There are certain actions that, if you were asked on a quiz, you would label them as inappropriate, immoral, or wrong. Yet each of us experience moments in life where, in the midst of difficult circumstances, these same decisions suddenly appear appropriate, moral, or even good.

Let's say you are attending the MTV Video Music Awards, and you desperately believe Beyoncé deserves to win a particular award, maybe "Best Female Video." Then you're forced to watch as the award is given to Taylor Swift.

That's a trial. That's a difficult moment to endure because you felt invested in Beyoncé's work. And as you are thinking about the injustice of it all, a thought slips into your mind: *I should go up there and interrupt Taylor while she's giving her acceptance speech. I should snatch the microphone away from her and chastise the MTV establishment for making this terrible mistake.*

That's temptation. It's when an option is presented to your mind that you know deep down is a bad idea, maybe an immoral idea, but in a particular moment it feels so *right*.

That's clearly a simple situation, but let's name some that may hit closer to home:

- Daily stress compounds and the voice in your head invites you to escape into alcohol or pornography.
- Intense desire to be liked by a certain crowd encourages you to compromise your moral values.
- Profound loneliness leads you to obsess about your body.
- Hurt feelings make lashing out at someone feel completely justified.

What kinds of temptations (food, entertainment, lust, etc.) are you good at resisting?

What kinds of temptations do you have trouble resisting?

Much of the power of temptation comes from its persistence. Temptation does not usually come like a single crashing wave but like the steady pull of an undertow. You don't even realize it has you until you are miles down shore, and it's pulling you out to sea. What do you do in that situation? You must be aware, and you must take action. The same is true in temptation. You must identify it, and then defeat it. Here's how.

SEE THE SOURCE

> "Let no one say when he is tempted, 'I am being tempted by God,' for God cannot be tempted with evil, and he himself tempts no one" (James 1:13).

Watch the *This Changes Everything* video for Session 3, available at *threadsmedia.com/thischangeseverything*.

THIS CHANGES EVERYTHING

What does James say about temptation in this verse? What's the source of temptation?

James begins by saying that we should never blame God when we experience temptation. We should never identify God as the source of our desire to do something wrong. I know people who do this. As a pastor I've had people say to me, "Ben, I know most Christians think this particular activity is a sin, but why would God give me these desires if He didn't want me to do something with them?" I've had people say that to me in connection with multiple issues, and my response is always the same: Do not blame God. Do not make God the culprit when you are tempted to do something you know is wrong.

Have you ever blamed God for tempting you, as if He put in you the desire to sin? If so, what were the circumstances?

Do you believe God tests us on purpose? What's the difference between being tested and being tempted?

Does God test us? Does He bring trials into our lives for specific purposes? Yes. He does that all the time. Look at Deuteronomy 8, for example:

> **"The whole commandment that I command you today you shall be careful to do, that you may live and multiply, and go in and possess the land that the LORD swore to give to your fathers. And you shall remember the whole way that the LORD your God has led you these forty years in the wilderness, that he might humble you, testing you to know what was in your heart, whether you would keep his commandments or not"** (vv. 1-2).

 In Job, all the calamity that befalls him comes only with the permission of the God who works all things according to the counsel of His will.

According to these verses, what was the test that God put the Israelites through? What was His purpose in doing so?

Now look at Genesis 2:

> "The LORD God took the man and put him in the garden of Eden to work it and keep it. And the LORD God commanded the man, saying, 'You may surely eat of every tree of the garden, but of the tree of the knowledge of good and evil you shall not eat, for in the day that you eat of it you shall surely die'" (vv. 15-17).

How did the tree of the knowledge of good and evil represent a test for Adam and Eve?

God will test you just like He tested Adam and Eve. He will put you in a difficult situation in order to see how you respond. God may even plant the tree of the knowledge of good and evil in your front yard, but He will never tell you to eat the fruit. He will never lean in close and whisper, "That fruit looks good; take a bite." It goes against His very nature.

So why does God test us? Let's look at Deuteronomy 8 again:

> "Take care lest you forget the LORD your God by not keeping his commandments and his rules and his statutes, which I command you today . . . who fed you in the wilderness with manna that your fathers did not know, that he might humble you and test you, to do you good in the end" (vv. 11,16).

Like a coach puts his players through drills to prepare them for the game, God tests us in order to make us better. Like a father disciplines his children for their good, God tests us for our good. Will God allow us to go through difficult circumstances? Count on it. Yet know that He does so to strengthen our faith, never to destroy it. Now let me be clear: I do not believe every trial we experience is simply a test from God. He will purpose or allow all manner of difficulties in our lives for a host of reasons. Sometimes He lets us see His designs in trial, and sometimes He does not. But what we can say is that every trial has within it the potential to teach us something—if we will allow it.

The Source of Temptation

So if God is not to blame for our temptation, who is? Where does temptation come from? Let's look back at James:

> "Let no one say when he is tempted, 'I am being tempted by God,' for God cannot be tempted with evil, and he himself tempts no one. But each person is tempted when he is lured and enticed by his own desire. Then desire when it has conceived gives birth to sin, and sin when it is fully grown brings forth death" (James 1:13-15).

Where does James say temptation comes from?

To put it simply, your temptations come from you.

God does not cause us to sin. Circumstances will never demand it either. Temptations always rise up from within ourselves. This leads to a natural question: How do I know when I am being tempted?

SEE HOW IT WORKS

I love the fishing imagery James used to describe how temptation works. When you go fishing, you drop a lure right in front of the fish you are trying to catch. Why? Because you want to grab its attention. You want the fish to see the lure and focus on it, because seeing the lure will stir its affections. You want the fish to think: *Oh my, look at that little frog. Look how it is swimming around in little circles—it looks injured and delicious!* You present a *lure* so you can *entice* the little fish. And when he makes the decision to enact the will—to bite down—then you've got him. He didn't even see the hook. You grabbed his attention and stirred his affections. And when he enacted the will, he became dinner.

James says the same kind of thing happens with us whenever we are tempted to sin. And we all know how that works, don't we? We all understand what it feels like to see the bait sitting out there and go, "Ooh, I want that."

Maybe you are currently single but not really happy about being single. You want to be in a meaningful relationship. Then you walk down the road and see a couple holding hands. Then you see the birds flying two-by-two. Then you start thinking about all your friends who are married or dating. And as these thoughts persist, an idea is solicited in your mind . . . and then you'll date a loser—someone you know does not care about the things of God. Yet you are so captivated by your desire to be with someone, you'll compromise. And after months of pain, you look up and realize you are somewhere you were never meant to be. How did it happen? Your mind was lured, your emotions enticed, and your will enacted.

Maybe you're skipping along through life and all of a sudden the thought enters your mind that you should look at naked people. And you realize you can access pictures of naked people on the phone in your hand. Or maybe you are going through a rough stretch emotionally. You are in a conflict or you are having trouble dealing with some problems, and you remember how everything kind of fuzzed out the last time you got drunk and you didn't have to think about those problems for a while.

It is temptation. It is a lure floating right there in front of our eyes, and we get so tempted by the opportunity to experience pleasure or avoid pain that we completely ignore the hook. We do not see the consequences—or we do not allow ourselves to think of the consequences—and we pay a price in the end.

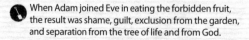
When Adam joined Eve in eating the forbidden fruit, the result was shame, guilt, exclusion from the garden, and separation from the tree of life and from God.

THIS CHANGES EVERYTHING

When have you felt tempted recently to do something you knew was sinful? What happened?

As a side note, I need to make sure it is clear that all of us experience temptation, but we are often tempted by different things. You may hear that one of your friends is struggling with a particular issue, and you may think, *I can't believe you are tempted by that.* You may even condemn that person in your heart because that specific issue is not a temptation for you and you do not understand how they could do something so terrible.

But that does not mean you are without lures. It just means something different needs to be presented in order to entice you. And rest assured—something will be coming sooner or later. There will be a temptation that's tailor-made for you, and then it will be your turn to struggle. The trick is knowing what kinds of lures have the potential to snag your attention.

That's why I advise you to spend as much time as possible working to understand yourself. Be a student of yourself and your own unique affections. Understand what causes you to feel tempted and then work on strategies to avoid those temptations and resist the ones you can't avoid.

What types of lures appeal to you?

What emotions do you experience most strongly after resisting temptation?

What emotions do you experience after failing to resist temptation?

 Satan tempted Jesus in an effort to divert Him from accomplishing God's mission on earth (see Matthew 4:1; Mark 1:12; Luke 4:3).

So after you've properly identified the *source* of your temptations and then have begun to recognize *how* it works, how can you keep from being swept up by them? How do you resist the lure?

SEE WHERE IT LEADS: SIN AND DEATH

To find the answers, look again at James 1:

> "But each person is tempted when he is lured and enticed by his own desire. Then desire when it has conceived gives birth to sin, and sin when it is fully grown brings forth death. Do not be deceived, my beloved brothers" (vv. 14-16).

Truth be told, James was not using fishing imagery. He had a different metaphor in mind: sex.

You may not catch the inference, but James's words here have a sexual nature. In the original language, the word James used for "desire" has a feminine form. His language is reminiscent of a famous passage in the Old Testament, Proverbs 7, where the father warns his son of the temptress. She will whisper seductive words and make promises that you will not get caught. Her lips promise delight, but her feet will lead you like an ox to the slaughter.

> "A woman came to meet him
> dressed like a prostitute,
> having a hidden agenda.
> She is loud and defiant;
> her feet do not stay at home.
> Now in the street, now in the squares,
> she lurks at every corner.
> She grabs him and kisses him;
> she brazenly says to him,
> 'I've made fellowship offerings;
> today I've fulfilled my vows.
> So I came out to meet you,
> to search for you, and I've found you.
> I've spread coverings on my bed—

THIS CHANGES EVERYTHING

richly colored linen from Egypt.
I've perfumed my bed
with myrrh, aloes, and cinnamon.
Come, let's drink deeply of lovemaking until morning.
Let's feast on each other's love!
My husband isn't home;
he went on a long journey.
He took a bag of money with him
and will come home at the time of the full moon.'
She seduces him with her persistent pleading;
she lures with her flattering talk.
He follows her impulsively
like an ox going to the slaughter,
like a deer bounding toward a trap
until an arrow pierces its liver,
like a bird darting into a snare—
he doesn't know it will cost him his life.
Now, my sons, listen to me,
and pay attention to the words of my mouth.
Don't let your heart turn aside to her ways;
don't stray onto her paths.
For she has brought many down to death;
her victims are countless.
Her house is the road to Sheol,
descending to the chambers of death" (Proverbs 7:10-27,
HCSB).

What do these verses teach about the nature of temptation?

What do these verses teach about the consequences of submitting to temptation?

According to James, the stirring up of our desires is not a sin. Temptation is not a sin. But when we allow ourselves to be seduced by our desires—when we submit to temptation—there is a consummation that happens. A union takes place. And when we join with our desires in that way, it conceives sin.

But it does not end there. Because once sin is born—once we've brought it forth and set it loose—it keeps expanding. It grows and develops until it becomes fully mature. And once our sin is fully mature, it produces death. This is shocking imagery, and that's exactly what James intended.

I can tell you from experience that one of the most joyful places on the planet is the delivery room. Seeing our little girl come into the world was a thrilling event. James takes that beautiful imagery and turns it into a horror film. You unite with desire, and she will give birth, but what she brings forth is not the joy of a new life; it is death.

In his autobiography, Johnny Cash recalls his first experience with mood-altering drugs: "I thought, *Boy, this is really something. This is the greatest thing in the world, to make you feel so good when it was hurting so bad. . . .*" Johnny then carried on a love affair with pills throughout many years of his career. He crashed numerous cars while high, once starting a forest fire that nearly wiped out an endangered species of California condor. By the age of 35 he stood six-foot, one-and-a-half-inch tall frame and weighed less than 155 pounds. The romance was killing him. He writes,

> "And as I've said before, all mood-altering drugs carry a demon called Deception. You think, *If this is so bad, why does it feel so good?* I used to tell myself, *God created this; it's got to be the greatest thing in the world.* But it's like the old saying about the wino: he starts by drinking out of the bottle, and then the bottle starts drinking out of him."[1]

So how do you battle temptation? Here's James's simple admonition: Before you take a ride with temptation, look down the road to see where it will take you. Or, to use James's imagery: Before you jump in bed with a given desire, see what kind of baby you will produce. I promise you, thousands of men and women who committed adultery would have resisted the romantic impulse of the moment if they had just paused long enough to imagine the devastation their indiscretion would cause down the road—a lost career, a ruined reputation, a broken family, and so forth. Johnny may have been spared years of pain and

 Choosing not to consider immediate and long-term consequences is a prescription for regret, guilt, and heartache. The sign of a mature person is that he or she takes time to think, reflect, and contemplate prior to action.

THIS CHANGES EVERYTHING

self-destruction if he had looked ahead and seen what drugs would ultimately do to his body and his relationships. Sin looks much less sexy when viewed in the bright light of day.

Let's consider the effects of just one common transgression: divorce. In an article for *Time* magazine, writer Caitlin Flanagan argues,

> "There is no other single force causing as much measurable hardship and human misery in this country as the collapse of marriage. . . . The reason for these appeals to lasting unions is simple: on every single significant outcome related to short-term well-being and long-term success, children from intact, two-parent families outperform those from single-parent households. Longevity, drug abuse, school performance and dropout rates, teen pregnancy, criminal behavior and incarceration — if you can measure it, a sociologist has; and in all cases, the kids living with both parents drastically outperform the others."[2]

What evidence can you see in today's culture of temptation leading to sin and ultimately to death?

Take a moment to evaluate your own temptations. Write down the strongest ones in your life at the moment.

When you give in to these desires, what does it ultimately produce? Does it ever bring forth the life you hoped?

Imagine yourself thinking about the end result in the midst of the temptation. How would it impact your decision-making in that moment?

LOOK UP

So we've seen the flow of temptation from its source, through its course, and to its ultimate destination. While this knowledge is helpful, it is only half the battle. Getting out of the wrong stream is only the first step.

> "Do not be deceived, my beloved brothers. Every good gift and every perfect gift is from above, coming down from the Father of lights with whom there is no variation or shadow due to change. Of his own will he brought us forth by the word of truth, that we should be a kind of firstfruits of his creatures" (James 1:16-18).

How does James describe God in these verses?

How does he describe us?

James implores us not to be deceived. Yet he does not simply mean fooled into believing destructive desires will bring life. James takes us a level deeper, talking about God's nature as a Father who cares for His children. Why? Because at the root of our temptation stands a failure to see God rightly. Our fundamental problem is not lust nor greed nor anger. Our fundamental problem is our theology. We've failed to believe that God cares and that He will take care of us.

> "Now the serpent was more crafty than any other beast of the field that the LORD God had made. He said to the woman, 'Did God actually say, "You shall not eat of any tree in the garden"?' And the

 James 1:17 refers to God, who created the lights that rule days and seasons (Genesis 1:14-19). God's nature is unchanging and His promises are secure.

woman said to the serpent, 'We may eat of the fruit of the trees in the garden, but God said, "You shall not eat of the fruit of the tree that is in the midst of the garden, neither shall you touch it, lest you die."' But the serpent said to the woman, 'You will not surely die. For God knows that when you eat of it your eyes will be opened, and you will be like God, knowing good and evil.' So when the woman saw that the tree was good for food, and that it was a delight to the eyes, and that the tree was to be desired to make one wise, she took of its fruit and ate, and she also gave some to her husband who was with her, and he ate. Then the eyes of both were opened, and they knew that they were naked. And they sewed fig leaves together and made themselves loincloths" (Genesis 3:1-7).

How did the serpent begin his argument with Eve? How did he shift her view of God? How did this misunderstanding of God lead her to give in to temptation?

Before the serpent could make the fruit look appealing, he first had to make God look unappealing. Only when I am convinced that God will not take care of me does temptation to look other places find its strength.

Think about it: Why are we tempted to indulge in sex outside of God's ordained, covenantal bond of marriage? Because we believe that if we submit to God's rules we will miss out on joy. Do you see the deception? In that moment, we join Eve in believing that God does not care about us, and that if we want satisfaction we must seek it apart from Him. This is where all temptation begins. So if we want to cut off the source of temptation's power, we must swing our ax here at the root. We must look at the Word of God to see who God truly is. We must fight to believe right things about Him. Here James reminds us that God is the Source of true joy. He's the One who gives us good things, and He's the One we can always count on because He never changes.

 A Jiu-Jitsu artist masters what they call "the squeeze." They slowly constrict their arms or legs around your neck so that you cannot escape, and then they squeeze until you give in or lose consciousness. It is the art of breaking your will. How do you get out of it? You must fight!

If we need proof, James reminds us that through His own will God "brought us forth by the word of truth, that we should be a kind of firstfruits of his creatures" (v. 18). "Brought forth" is birthing imagery. God's giving birth in this passage, too! What did God bring forth? Us. Jesus came into this sin-filled world and died for our benefit—He sacrificed Himself so we could be born again and experience new and better life. And that is just the beginning!

We look up to see that God is the Source of all good things. Not only that, He is leading all of history toward life! One day God will do the same thing with all of creation. In Revelation 21 He says, "Behold, I am making all things new" (v. 5). But it starts with us. We are the firstfruits. As we are born again and receive the good gift of eternal life, we become evidence throughout the universe of God's goodness and the restoration that will come to all things.

Just as important, we become witnesses for those struggling here on earth—including ourselves. When you see God making people new, even though they're lost in sin, you can look at your particular situation and say: "God will make this new even though it is hard. And I will not believe the lie. I will fight to believe the truth. And I will cling to God even in the dark, believing the sun will rise."

LIVE IT OUT

Maybe you are feeling discouraged right now because you've already done that. You are thinking: *I'm born again, but I've still got problems. I still do not know how to handle this relationship. I still do not know how to deal with this stress. I'm still a mess in these areas. I still have these addictions. I still have these lusts. If this radical new creation happened, why am I still such a mess?*

Those are good questions. Let me close out this session by highlighting two final pieces of practical advice from James. These can help us understand the process of moving closer and closer to the people we want to be.

First, James says we need to humble ourselves and listen.

 Take a moment to identify the coping mechanisms (responses to and handling of stress) modeled by your family. What things proved helpful? What things were harmful?

THIS CHANGES EVERYTHING

> "Know this, my beloved brothers: let every person be quick to hear, slow to speak, slow to anger; for the anger of man does not produce the righteousness of God" (James 1:19-20).

One of the reasons some Christians aren't growing and maturing spiritually is that they're proud. They're arrogant. They're quick to anger because they still view the world as something that should do what *they* want—and oftentimes they even view God as Someone who should behave how they want Him to behave.

Do you have an easy or hard time controlling your anger? How might your frustration in a given moment be an indicator of pride in your heart?

Do you believe that you are "slow to speak"? Why or why not?

Instead of acting as if we are in charge of the universe, James instructs us:

> "Therefore put away all filthiness and rampant wickedness and receive with meekness the implanted word, which is able to save your souls" (v. 21).

See the word "implanted"? It is the pregnancy thing again. We've got the Word of God planted inside us to help us grow and mature, but we'll never be able to access its power unless we approach things with a spirit of meekness rather than arrogance and pride.

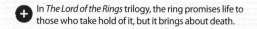 In *The Lord of the Rings* trilogy, the ring promises life to those who take hold of it, but it brings about death.

That's the first reason we do not grow as quickly as we'd like. The second reason is simply that we fail to do what we know we are supposed to do. We go to church and read the Bible and fill our minds with spiritual things—but that intellectual knowledge never changes the way we act.

James says that's a bad idea:

> "But be doers of the word, and not hearers only, deceiving your-selves. For if anyone is a hearer of the word and not a doer, he is like a man who looks intently at his natural face in a mirror. For he looks at himself and goes away and at once forgets what he was like. But the one who looks into the perfect law, the law of liberty, and perseveres, being no hearer who forgets but a doer who acts, he will be blessed in his doing" (vv. 22-25).

How are we to approach the Word? What should be our response to reading the Word?

I love the illustration James uses to finish making his point. He says when you encounter God's Word, do not approach it like a man approaches a mirror. You know what he's talking about, right? Most guys glance over at a mirror, give a little flex, and then walk away. It is a fleeting and superficial encounter.

Instead, James says we need to approach God's Word the same way that most women approach a mirror. Because when a woman stations herself in front of a mirror, she does so with the expectation that something needs to change. She looks intently at herself in order to see what can be adjusted or improved, and then she works diligently. She transforms herself.

That's how we need to approach God's Word if we want to experience growth and maturity in the Christian life. Study Scripture intently. Do not read the Bible and go, "Oh, that was fascinating," and then live your life however you think makes the most sense. No, receive God's Word and let it change you. Let it transform you.

APPLY TO LIFE

> **REFLECT:** In the great allegory *The Pilgrim's Progress,* the main character, Christian, must journey through the Valley of the Shadow of Death. While there the Devil blocks his path and entices him to abandon his journey toward heaven. When Christian resists the temptation, a battle ensues. Resisting temptation proves difficult for Christian, and at one moment he's critically wounded. As the Enemy approaches to deliver a mortal blow, Christian draws out the Sword of Truth and uses it to vanquish his enemy. He rises and encounters a friend and, as they quote the truth of God's Word together, the tempters in the valley flee. The Word of God is not only a mirror to examine yourself with and a plant, rooted and growing inside of you. It is also a weapon.

> **LISTEN:** Purchase "Whom Shall I Fear (God of Angel Armies)" by Chris Tomlin, "Make War" by Tedashii, and "Abide With Me" by Matthew Perryman Jones from the *This Changes Everything* playlist. Add these to your regular mix of music throughout the week to stay strong in the face of temptation.

NOTES

FAITH AND WORK

"What good is it, my brothers, if someone says he has faith but does not have works? Can that faith save him? If a brother or sister is poorly clothed and lacking in daily food, and one of you says to them, 'Go in peace, be warmed and filled,' without giving them the things needed for the body, what good is that? So also faith by itself, if it does not have works, is dead. But someone will say, 'You have faith and I have works.' Show me your faith apart from your works, and I will show you my faith by my works."

James 2:14-18

What's your initial reaction to these verses? Why?

Which words and phrases stand out to you most? Take a moment to circle them in the text.

I grew up going to church camp every summer. Amid all the crazy games, awkward flirting, periodic vandalism, and tearful hugs, two messages came across loud and clear. First, that a relationship with God is a free gift I cannot earn. It comes only by trusting in Jesus. Second, I should be sinning a whole lot less than I am right now. I need to work harder.

It wasn't until years later that I began to question how exactly those two messages related to each other. If a relationship with God is free, then why am I supposed to do or not do certain things? If I can't earn God's love or do anything to make Him love me more, then why should I work so hard to do the things He wants me to do?

Have you ever asked questions like this? It's not a bad thing to do. In fact, it is a healthy way to examine the faith, and it's exactly what James calls us to do in James 2:14-16.

In this session, we will examine the connection between faith and works. But to do this, we cannot simply look at James's words alone. In tackling this passage we must address a glaring issue in our Bible. Namely, it appears that James and Paul, the apostle who wrote much of the New Testament, are completely at odds on this topic.

Before we go any further, try explaining in your own words the relationship between faith and works.

JAMES VS. PAUL?

You can really feel the tension when you place Romans 3 and James alongside one another:

> **"For we hold that one is justified by faith apart from works of the law" (Romans 3:28).**

> **"You see that a person is justified by works and not by faith alone" (James 2:24).**

Call me crazy, but these verses seem to be saying the exact opposite of each other. Reading them together like this makes one naturally ask the question,

Watch the *This Changes Everything* video for Session 4, available at *threadsmedia.com/thischangeseverything*.

THIS CHANGES EVERYTHING

"Which is it?" Are we justified by faith apart from works or by works and not by faith alone? They can't both be right, can they? Some might go so far as to say, "They cannot both be true, therefore the Bible contradicts itself. Therefore the Bible is not the Word of God. Therefore Christianity is a lie, and I'm officially done with this Bible study!"

Before you freak out, we need to consider two historical facts. First, the early church embraced the teachings of both James and Paul. They had no problem with both books being included in the New Testament. So somehow they reconciled the writings of these two men. Second, James and Paul knew each other. Not only were they acquaintances, they were both major players in the first church council that gathered in Jerusalem specifically to address the relationship of faith and works! Both men participated in the council, and they walked away with consensus. So these guys agreed with each other. We just need to figure out how, because it does not sound like they do! And, more importantly, we need clarity on this issue because James states that there is a kind of faith that's worthless. We do not want that.

The best way to engage this topic is to examine how Paul explained the connection between faith and works and then consider James's approach. Two issues will help our conversation: words and content. (Nod to John Piper for some of these ideas![1])

Same Word, Different Meaning

Issue 1: We must keep in mind that a single word can carry a number of different meanings. Think of the word *rock,* for example. If I say "rock," I could be talking about a stone. I could be talking about a kind of music. I could be using it as a compliment, like "You rock!" I could be using it as a verb, as in something you do in a rocking chair. So in order to understand what I mean when I use the word *rock,* you need to hear the context in which I use it.

The same thing is happening between Paul and James when it comes to the word *justify,* which can actually mean a couple different things. First, to justify something can mean to make it right—to make it OK. If you have a debt, you can make it right by paying back the money you owe; you can justify the debt.

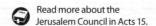
Read more about the
Jerusalem Council in Acts 15.

But the word *justify* can also mean to prove yourself right, or to show something to be right. So if you tell me something and I say, "justify that statement," I'm not telling you to make the statement true. I'm calling you to give me evidence that what you said is true. I'm asking you to vindicate it, to show it to be what it really is.

Same Meaning, Different Words
Issue 2: Sometimes the same meaning can be communicated using very different words. For example, if I talk about "soccer" and an English guy talks about "football," we're actually describing the same sport even though we are using different terms. It's the same game. As we'll see, Paul and James used a number of different words to describe faith and salvation, but they were actually arriving at the same ideas.

So what do these men believe about the relationship between faith and works? Let's begin with Paul.

PAUL'S VIEW
We will emphasize two aspects of Paul's view of the relationship between faith and works.

1. Paul argued that we are justified by faith alone.
Paul preached that a person is brought into a right relationship with God by faith alone with no basis whatsoever in works. As stated earlier in Romans 3:28, Paul declared that we are "justified by faith apart from works of the law." He then used Abraham as an argument, quoting Genesis 15: "Abraham believed God, and it was counted to him as righteousness" (Romans 4:3). But what does Paul mean by "justified"? He clarifies his intention in Romans 4:

> **"And to the one who does not work but believes in him who justifies the ungodly, his faith is counted as righteousness, just as David also speaks of the blessing of the one to whom God counts righteousness apart from works:**

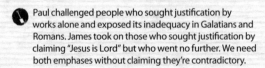

Paul challenged people who sought justification by works alone and exposed its inadequacy in Galatians and Romans. James took on those who sought justification by claiming "Jesus is Lord" but who went no further. We need both emphases without claiming they're contradictory.

THIS CHANGES EVERYTHING

'Blessed are those whose lawless deeds are forgiven,
    and whose sins are covered;
blessed is the man against whom the Lord will not count
    his sin'" (vv. 5-8).

So what is justification in this context? God (1) forgives lawless deeds and does not count their sin against them, and (2) He counts them as righteous. In other words, He removes something and He gives something. He cancels the penalty of sin. The person is forgiven. Guilt and condemnation are removed.

But He doesn't stop there.

God does not hold grudges. When a person is justified, God forgives *and* He credits or counts them as right with God. He declares them to be in right standing with Him. The relationship is clear. It's good. So sin is removed and a right standing before God is given.

How does someone receive this? Paul states again and again that it is "by faith" and not based on any work that they've done!

But faith in what? Paul makes that clear in Romans 5:

> "Therefore, since we have been justified by faith, we have peace with God through our Lord Jesus Christ. Through him we have also obtained access by faith into this grace in which we stand, and we rejoice in hope of the glory of God" (vv. 1-2).

We are justified (declared right) with God, and therefore have peace with God. In other words, He is no longer angry with us over our sin. How did we arrive in this place? By faith in our Lord Jesus Christ who gives us access to the Father. It was through the work of Jesus, not our own work!

➕ *Justification*—right relationship between God and man (see Romans 5:1). God establishes this relationship through Christ, so that it is not merely a temporary state that can be destroyed by man's actions but a state that results in eternal peace between the redeemed and the Redeemer.

2. Paul believed God puts His Spirit inside of us and that Spirit moves us to love.
There was a popular bumper sticker back in the day that read, "Christians aren't perfect, just forgiven." That's actually not right at all! We are far more than "just forgiven." Paul declares in Galatians 3:26 that Christians are "sons of God through faith in Christ Jesus" (HCSB). We are not just forgiven; we are declared family! He goes further: "because you are sons, God has sent the Spirit of his Son into our hearts, crying, 'Abba! Father!'" (Galatians 4:6). God did not simply remove the guilt of our sin. He removed it, and then He put His very Spirit inside of us!

Once the Spirit of God gets in us, He begins to work. He transforms us. He changes us from the inside-out in a process we usually refer to as sanctification. Paul commanded us to "work out your own salvation with fear and trembling, *for it is God who works in you,* both to will and to work for His good pleasure" (Philippians 2:12-13, emphasis mine).

The greatest evidence of our growth through the Holy Spirit is that we begin to demonstrate the fruit of love. Paul wrote: "For in Christ Jesus neither circumcision nor uncircumcision counts for anything, but only faith working through love" (Galatians 5:6).

Read Galatians 5:22-25. What kinds of fruit does the Spirit produce in us?

How have you experienced this type of spiritual growth in recent years?

Notice what Paul says: What counts with God? Faith. What kind of faith? Faith that "works through love" (see Galatians 5:6). He doesn't say that what counts is faith plus a layer of loving works added to faith. He says that what counts with God is *the kind of faith that by its nature produces love.* But it is faith that gives us our right standing with God. The love that comes from it only shows that it is in fact, real, living, justifying faith. True faith in God will express itself in deeds. It will never be "alone," meaning, without some expression.

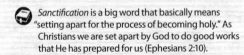 *Sanctification* is a big word that basically means "setting apart for the process of becoming holy." As Christians we are set apart by God to do good works that He has prepared for us (Ephesians 2:10).

THIS CHANGES EVERYTHING

That's a very basic look at what Paul wants us to understand about salvation. We are saved by faith alone, and having "believed in him, were sealed with the promised Holy Spirit" (Ephesians 1:13). The Spirit then begins to work in us so that our faith works itself out in love. Faith becomes love. That's Paul's gospel.

JAMES'S VIEW

Here's the great news: James says the exact same thing! Although he uses different language and approaches things from a different angle, the primary idea is the same: Faith works itself out in love.

1. James believed in salvation by grace through faith!
Let's look at the big question: Did James teach that people are saved by works? No! He made it clear that we are born again by God's grace through faith in Him. Read James 1:17-18:

> **"Every good gift and every perfect gift is from above, coming down from the Father of lights with whom there is no variation or shadow due to change. Of his own will he brought us forth by the word of truth, that we should be a kind of firstfruits of his creatures."**

We are born into God's family! Just like Paul and John and Jesus said! You didn't help out in your physical birth. You didn't contribute at all. Mom did all the work. It is the same with your spiritual birth. You didn't do "works" to become God's child. He brought you forth by waking you up to the truth!

Now look at James 2:5:

> **"Listen, my beloved brothers, has not God chosen those who are poor in the world to be rich in faith and heirs of the kingdom, which he has promised to those who love him?"**

What's the definition of an heir?

 "Let the water and the blood, From Thy
wounded side which flowed, Be of sin the double
cure, Save from wrath and make me pure."
—Augustus M. Toplady, "Rock of Ages, Cleft for Me"[2]

Based on this definition, what can you conclude about how we enter the kingdom of God?

There is a vast difference between earning something and receiving an inheritance. I had to pay my way through college. For four years I mowed lawns, waited tables, and served as a parking garage attendant to scrounge and save to pay the bills. Once I had to survive for two weeks on nothing but a box of Bisquick®!

My wife, on the other hand, had a wealthy grandmother who set up a college fund for her grandchildren. Donna, as an heir, did not have to work for her education. She freely received it as a gift because that's what heirs do. An heir does not earn their inheritance. They receive it. Here James calls the Christian an heir of God's kingdom! We do not work for or earn our salvation! Thus James, like Paul, declares that we're saved by the grace of God through faith.

2. James believed that faith works!
Also like Paul, James held that saving faith always manifests itself in works of love. Notice what he says in verse 14, and see if it matches the content of Paul:

> **"What good is it, my brothers, if someone says he has faith but does not have works? Can that faith save him?"**

The form of the question assumes a negative answer. No. That kind of faith cannot save him. According to James, there exists a kind of faith that some may have that does not work. James condemns this kind of faith as worthless. Why? Because true faith, in Paul's explanation, works itself out though love! This is exactly what you see in verses 15 and 16. Notice James's illustration:

> **"If a brother or sister is poorly clothed and lacking in daily food, and one of you says to them, 'Go in peace, be warmed and filled,' without giving them the things needed for the body, what good is that?"**

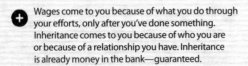 Wages come to you because of what you do through your efforts, only after you've done something. Inheritance comes to you because of who you are or because of a relationship you have. Inheritance is already money in the bank—guaranteed.

THIS CHANGES EVERYTHING

Answer: It's not good at all! True love does not simply wish someone well. Love sacrifices for those in need. The apostle John said it this way:

> "If anyone has the world's goods and sees his brother in need, yet closes his heart against him, how does God's love abide in him?" (1 John 3:17).

John cannot conceive of a love for God that fails to become love for others! James agrees. He concludes his illustration by declaring,

> "So also faith by itself, if it does not have works, is dead" (James 2:17).

By this James does not mean that we're saved by works plus faith. Rather, he was explaining that the kind of faith that saves will naturally produce acts of love.

SIGNS OF TRUE FAITH

Conversations like this often naturally lead us to wonder: *OK, so if true faith becomes love, how do I know if I have the real stuff? Do I have to be a perfectly loving person in every moment of the day?* No. James makes it clear in chapter 3 that "we all stumble in many ways" (v. 2). If flawless behavior is not the requirement to know that you belong to God, then how do we know? James offers us four signs. The first two do not necessarily prove that we have true faith. The second pair of signs does indicate that one possesses genuine faith. Let's explore all four.[3]

The two signs that don't necessarily prove one has genuine faith are in James 2:

> "You believe that God is one; you do well. Even the demons believe—and shudder! (v. 19)".

First, James explains that knowing sound doctrine does not guarantee that one has genuine faith. The belief that "God is one" stood as the foundation of all proper knowledge of God (Deuteronomy 6:4). James declares that a person does well to know this truth about the nature of God. It's a great thing to know good theology! Yet we can ace a religious studies test and still not truly know God. How can we say this? Simply stated: "Even the demons believe." Demons know right things about God. They know more about Him than all of us! They were there when He fashioned the world! However, I think we would all agree that demons are not God's kids. Knowledge alone does not make one a child of God.

Second, notice that the demons "shudder." They not only believe in God, they respect His power. They quake when they contemplate His might. Yet again, this does not make them children of God! Many people possess some level of respect for the power of God. They avoid cussing in church, or they bow their heads when others pray. Yet, according to James, possessing a healthy respect of God's power does not necessarily mean one has genuine faith.

Now, a person who knows God will possess both of these things. They will know right things about God and they will respect Him. Yet these attributes do not tell us conclusively that we are His.[4]

Why don't these signs guarantee genuine faith?

So what are sure signs that we belong to God? How do we know we are His?

The first we have already talked about: True faith always manifests itself in a love for people. It moves us to care for widows and orphans. It guides us to respect our brothers and sisters in lowly positions.

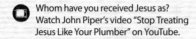
Whom have you received Jesus as?
Watch John Piper's video "Stop Treating Jesus Like Your Plumber" on YouTube.

THIS CHANGES EVERYTHING

The second sign of genuine faith is that it manifests itself in a deep love for God. This is where the two men, Paul and James, converge. To prove their points about the nature of justification before God, both men use Abraham as an example. James will do it here, and Paul in Romans 4. This makes sense. The Bible calls Abraham the father of the faith (see Luke 16:22-31; Romans 3:27–4:25). So if you want to answer a question about faith, it's wise to reference the original guy!

James references two events in Abraham's life. In Genesis 15:5, God reaffirms His promise to Abraham that He will give him a host of descendants through his barren wife. Abraham believes God, and James records the outcome:

> **"Abraham believed God, and it was reckoned to him as righteousness" (James 2:23).**

God declared Abraham to be righteous! Had Abraham lived a perfect life? Not at all. So why did God call him right? Because Abraham trusted the promise God had made that He would give Abe descendants, through whom the world would be blessed.

In Romans 4:3 Paul points to this same moment in Abraham's life to prove his point as well. Only one thing causes God to declare someone righteous: faith. Abraham believed God and God counted that as righteousness. So how are you made right with God? Only by trusting in God, not by any work.

Then James highlights another moment in Abraham's life. In James 2:21 he fast-forwards to a moment 30 years after the events of Genesis 15. In Genesis 22 we are told that "God tested Abraham" by commanding him to offer up his son Isaac as a sacrifice.

What was God testing? Abraham's faith. What was God looking for? Actions that prove that Abraham's faith, which he expressed years before, was genuine. So the issue in James 2:21 is not that first act of justification that put Abraham in right standing with God. The issue is the test: was Abraham's faith the living kind that produces "the obedience of faith" (Romans 16:26) or the dead kind that has no effect on life?

 Abraham means "father of a multitude." He was the first Hebrew patriarch who became known as the prime example of faith.[5]

Notice how James explains what happened in that moment in Abraham's life:

> **"Was not Abraham our father justified by works when he offered up his son Isaac on the altar? You see that faith was active along with his works, and faith was completed by his works; and the Scripture was fulfilled that says, 'Abraham believed God, and it was counted to him as righteousness'—and he was called a friend of God" (James 2:21-23).**

Let me point out a few critical facts: First, "justified" in verse 21 cannot mean "declare to be righteous," because that happened in Abraham's life 30 years before! This passage uses *justify* in the second sense. God designed this test to show or prove that Abraham's faith, which he had held for three decades, was indeed the real stuff.

Second, notice in verse 22 that Abraham's faith was an active force in his works. This was not a religious act that Abraham performed to add extra merit to his faith. Rather, his faith proved to be an animating power behind his acts. His faith produced action.

Third, notice again in verse 22 that Abraham's works completed his faith. The word *completed* means "to be brought to maturity or perfection." To borrow Paul's language, Abraham's faith worked through love (see Galatians 5:6).

How was Abraham's act a display of love? When God saw that Abraham trusted Him completely, even to the point of offering up his only son (believing that God would somehow spare his son's life, see Hebrews 11:17-19), God declared "Now I know that you love Me" (see Genesis 22:12). Abraham's faith worked itself out as a loving act toward God, declaring by his actions that he believed that God is worth trusting in any circumstance. This is far more than simply attending religious services. Abraham's act proved that he truly trusted the Lord. This is the greatest sign that we have true saving faith. True faith in God works itself out as love for God! It trusts God's heart and honors God with its actions.

 James recognizes that Christians continue to sin (see James 3:2), so he clearly does not expect us to have 100 percent conformity to the will of God. We are still sinners under the grace of God.

THIS CHANGES EVERYTHING

What does trusting and honoring God look like on a daily basis?

True faith displays itself in (1) genuine love toward others and, (2) genuine love for God. Notice James points out that Abraham was called a friend of God. A friend is not someone you fear or do things for because you feel like you have to. A friend is someone you enjoy being with. They are someone whom you love for who they are.

This is what the true believer possesses that the demons cannot! Demons may have right theology. They may have a proper fear of God's majesty. But what they lack is a heart that sees God as lovely. They don't love God. How do you know you are a Christian? You love Christ. How do you know you are saved? You cherish the Savior.

God's people do not simply fear Him. They do not perform religious acts to avoid His wrath. True faith is a friendship with God. It enjoys God. And as we love and trust Him, He will always aim us toward loving others.

JUSTIFICATION: PAUL AND JAMES

When Paul says that we are justified by faith, and not works, he means that God *declares* us to be righteous because of the finished work of Christ and we can't do anything to add to that. James would agree: when we are brought forth by the word of truth we are heirs to the kingdom promised to those who love Him.

When James says we are justified by works he means that our actions show that our conversion is legitimate. True faith manifests itself in love for God and others. Paul would agree: all that matters is "faith working through love" (Galatians 5:6).

So what shall we make of the apparent contradiction in James and Paul? Let me summarize it this way: Several years ago I got into an argument with a buddy

 If you claim faith but are totally unconcerned with obedience, you should spend some time questioning your faith.

of mine about where to find the best beef jerky in Texas. (Yes, here in the Lone Star State we do debate this sort of thing.) I informed my friend that the Hillje Smokehouse on Highway 59 sells jerky that will literally change your life.

Needless to say I was shocked when my friend responded: "No. There is another place on 59 called Prasek's, and it is far and away the best beef jerky on the planet." I tried to reason with her. I calmly explained that if she had ever tried the jerky from Hillje's, she would understand that she was presently embarrassing herself by speaking with such ignorance. She disagreed, marshaling her best arguments for the supremacy of Prasek's. We argued back and forth for quite a long time. We had no peace in our friendship.

Eventually we took a trip down Highway 59 together, to put an end to this Great Jerky Debate. It was with great anticipation that we approached the general area we had been discussing—we both felt like we were about to be vindicated. Imagine our surprise, then, when we turned a corner and saw a big sign advertising Prasek's Hillje Smokehouse.

Turns out Prasek was the owner's name, Hillje was the town, and the entire time my friend and I had been talking about the same jerky!

I tell that story because it illustrates the absurdity of the argument that Paul and James were advocating different views on salvation. In reality, Paul and James were two guys talking about the same doctrine—the same salvation.

I'll wrap up by giving both an encouragement and a challenge. The process of spiritual growth is a struggle. Living the Christian life can be difficult, and all of us will stumble in many ways. But you can know that if you've put your faith in Jesus Christ, you are going to be all right.

"And I am sure of this, that he who began a good work in you will bring it to completion at the day of Jesus Christ" (Philippians 1:6).

At the same time, we all need to be students of our own lives. As you look at your life, do you see faith working itself out in love? Do you see good works that positively influence the people in your community? Do you see a spiritual journey that's marked by growth?

These questions are vital to a healthy relationship with God. Fortunately, we'll be exploring these kinds of questions (and more) in the pages to come.

APPLY TO LIFE

> **CONNECT:** Are you carrying a heavy burden of guilt? If you've asked God's forgiveness and repented, He has forgotten it—and so should you. Talk to a wise friend about your burden. Ask God to help you accept what He's already forgiven.

> **STUDY:** For further study on the tension between faith and works, consider reading *Basic Christianity* by John Stott or *Mere Christianity* by C.S. Lewis.

> **LISTEN:** Purchase "Rock of Ages" by David Crowder Band and "Where Would We Be" by Matt Redman from the *This Changes Everything* playlist. Add these to your regular mix of music to keep "faith working through love" fresh on your mind this week.

NOTES

THE WEIGHT OF WORDS

"For we all stumble in many ways. And if anyone does not stumble in what he says, he is a perfect man, able also to bridle his whole body. If we put bits into the mouths of horses so that they obey us, we guide their whole bodies as well. Look at the ships also: though they are so large and are driven by strong winds, they are guided by a very small rudder wherever the will of the pilot directs. So also the tongue is a small member, yet it boasts of great things. . . . For every kind of beast and bird, of reptile and sea creature, can be tamed and has been tamed by mankind, but no human being can tame the tongue. It is a restless evil, full of deadly poison. With it we bless our Lord and Father, and with it we curse people who are made in the likeness of God. From the same mouth come blessing and cursing. My brothers, these things ought not to be so."

James 3:2-5a,7-10

A few years ago I read Sebastian Junger's book *Fire*. It discusses the world's most dangerous jobs. Can you guess what they are? Smoke jumpers stood out to me as one of the coolest. These guys parachute alone into forest fires to put them out by chopping down the burning trees. Then they hike out, which can take days. Whale hunting struck me as one of the most insane professions on the list. The International Whaling Commission permits the men on Bequia island in the Caribbean to take two humpback whales a year. If you're worried about the whales, let me explain their method of hunting: A five-man crew sets out in a small wooden sailboat called the "Why Ask" armed with a single spear. A 170-pound man versus a 40-ton whale—whom would you bet on? The surprise dangerous job entry: tree limbers. Seriously? Yes. It makes sense if you think about it: Climbing trees + carrying chainsaws = not healthy.

As entertaining as the book is, it omits one of the most terrifying jobs on the planet: Bible teacher. Don't believe me? Listen to James, the brother of Jesus, because he clearly sounds the warning:

> **"Not many of you should become teachers, my brothers . . ."** **(James 3:1a).**

As much as James treasured the truth, he warned his people that they should not rush to get on a stage and begin speaking. I agree with him. I tell young men this all the time. Why? What makes it so scary? A fear of public speaking? Not according to James. Something far more terrifying stands behind James's warning:

> **". . . for you know that we who teach will be judged with greater strictness" (v. 1b).**

Don't get me wrong; the world needs teachers. Paul told the Ephesians that God made some to be teachers, "to equip the saints for the work of ministry, for building up the body of Christ" (Ephesians 4:12). It's a risk that many have, and should, take—including James himself. So why does he warn his people not to rush into it?

First, teachers will receive stricter judgment. Notice James says that we know this. How do we know it? James was pointing back to what Jesus told us:

> **"Everyone to whom much was given, of him much will be required, and from him to whom they entrusted much, they will demand the more" (Luke 12:48b).**

In the words of Spiderman, "With great power comes great responsibility." We know this to be true. A car has much greater power than a bicycle. If you wreck a bike, you may get a lecture from your dad. If you wreck a car, you could kill someone. So we have stricter rules on who can drive, and harsher penalties if those laws are broken. If you've been given that awesome responsibility, you are held to a higher standard.

Watch the *This Changes Everything* video for Session 5, available at *threadsmedia.com/thischangeseverything*.

THIS CHANGES EVERYTHING

Teaching is like this. When you stand in front of a group of people—be it a crowd of thousands or a room of five—and you say, "Thus says the Lord," you wield enormous influence, and God will hold you accountable to that.

I regularly encounter people who want to be teachers because they are smart, funny, or ambitious. They are drawn to the attention that comes from being on a stage. If that's you, then beg God right now to keep you out of the spotlight. You need a holy fear of Him before you take up His Word to speak to them.

Take a moment to assess your life: Who are the people you influence?

How have you handled that power responsibly? In what ways have you not?

THE POWER OF THE TONGUE

James continues with a second reason why teaching is so dangerous. Not only must the teacher be mindful to wield his influence with care, he must do this while standing in front of a crowd and attempting to control the most dangerous organ in the human body: the tongue!

> **"For we all stumble in many ways. And if anyone does not stumble in what *he says,* he is a perfect man, able also to *bridle* his *whole body*" (James 3:2, emphasis mine).**

Do you agree that the tongue is the most difficult part of your body to control? Why or why not?

James admits that every human being will fail. We all—teacher or not—will struggle in a variety of ways. Some will battle to control lust. Others will fight to get a handle on anger. Some will wrestle against a propensity to judge others. Many will achieve victory over particular areas of struggle and will be an inspiration to us all. Yet James says if you can find someone who can get a handle on what he *says* (literally does not stumble "in words"), then you've just found a perfect human being. If you can get a handle on your mouth, then any other sinful impulse in any other part of your body will be easy to reign in. That is a bold statement. How can James speak that way?

James laid out his thesis: If you can control the tongue, then you can control any part of your life. Now he backs it up with two arguments.

THE TONGUE IS POWERFUL: LITTLE LEADS THE BIG

Your tongue controls the direction of your life. The little leads the big. James proves this point with three illustrations.

> **"If we put bits into the mouths of horses so that they obey us, we guide their whole bodies as well" (v. 3).**

What verbal links do you see between verses 2 and 3?

Try stating James's argument in your own words.

Have you ever seen a horse up close? Have you felt the ground shake when one galloped by? Horses are huge! The average horse weighs between 800 and 1,100 pounds. The average bit weighs less than 1 pound. Yet place one of those little pieces of metal in the mouth of a horse and you can lead that behemoth anywhere you want to go. Little girls can guide massive stallions if they can just get control of the horse's mouth. The little leads the big.

Verse 4 makes the same point:

> **"Look at the ships also: though they are *so large* and are driven by *strong* winds, they are guided by a *very small* rudder wherever the will of the pilot directs"** (emphasis mine).

The same idea holds true with a ship on the open sea. No matter how large a ship may be and no matter how powerful its engines, a comparatively tiny rudder will always control the ship. Why? You guessed it, because the little leads the big. The same is true of the tongue.

> **"So also the tongue is a small member, yet it boasts of great things"** (v. 5a).

The tongue is little, but it can make a great boast: It leads our lives, like a bit leads a horse or a rudder leads a ship. Think about it: The right word choice will land you a job. The wrong words will lose you a job. Recently, a sportscaster made some offhanded, racist remarks during a segment on ESPN. He no longer works for ESPN.

A few years ago a congressman from South Carolina yelled two words during a speech by the president: "You lie." The next week he received more than $2 million in donations. That's a million dollars a word.

Think about your own life. A well-placed compliment will start a friendship. An offhanded remark can damage a friendship. Our words will determine the course of our lives. The little leads the big.

Have you seen this principle play out in your own life? Have you ever said something that got you in trouble? Have you ever said something that won you special recognition? Explain.

In what ways has the course of your life been impacted by your speech?

At this point James has argued that if you can control the tongue you can control any part of your life. That's because your tongue has power to lead your entire life. This is only half the story. The tongue is powerful, but that power itself has the potential to produce disastrous consequences.

THE TONGUE IS DANGEROUS: BIG CONSEQUENCES

Read the remainder of verse 5:

> "How great a forest is set ablaze by such a small fire!"

On June 24, 2007, a wildfire broke loose in the Angora neighborhood of California. The fire burned "approximately 3,100 acres and destroyed 254 homes and 67 commercial structures."[1] The blaze caused in excess of $140 million in damages. Before everything was said and done, more than 2,000 firefighters were called to put their lives at risk in order to get the flames under control.

What caused this disaster? An illegal campfire, possibly lit by a discarded cigarette. A single careless act resulted in chaos on a massive scale.

Words are like this. The potential for damage is incalculable. Yet James does not stop here. The tongue doesn't simply possess the potential to produce evil; it *is* evil! It doesn't just contain the possibility of lighting a fire; it *is* a fire, a hellfire!

> "And the tongue is a fire, a world of unrighteousness. The tongue is set among our members, staining the whole body, setting on fire the entire course of life, and set on fire by hell" (v. 6).

James never wasted time with subtlety. The tongue not only has the potential to do damage; it will. Your tongue will corrupt everything in your body and set your whole life on fire. This is not the good kind of Holy-Spirit-passion-for-Jesus fire, either. Your tongue will light up your life with the fire of hell.

Little words can do great damage.

If you're walking down the street and three pretty girls smile at you and then a group of girls makes fun of you, which memory sticks in your mind? If you walk in and catch friends talking bad about you, even if they apologize, their words still linger.

Do you remember that rhyme we would say as kids when someone hurt our feelings? "Sticks and stones may break my bones, but words will never hurt me."

That is such a lie! Think about the moments when you said that to someone: Why did you say it? You repeated that little rhyme exactly *because* what someone just said to you hurt your feelings! Words can hurt us—and the wrong kinds of words will almost always hurt us. We know this because we've all experienced it.

When have you been positively affected by a person's words in recent months?

When have you been wounded by a person's words in recent months?

Do you find yourself more often encouraged or wounded by the speech of others?

Charles Spurgeon, known as the "Prince of Preachers," moved his congregation to Royal Surrey Gardens, a 10,000-seat music hall. During the first service on October 19, 1856, someone yelled "Fire!" The crowd panicked, and in the crush to escape, seven people were trampled to death. Spurgeon almost lost his mind with grief.[2]

For some of us, our perception of self has been dominated by careless words spoken by a family member. Some of us remember getting into fistfights with friends and then making up afterward. The bruises healed, and even a day or two later we may have laughed about it. But hurtful words can linger for years, even after an apology has been offered and accepted. If we're going to be accurate, we need to adapt the phrase, "Sticks and stones may break my bones, but words will burn this whole thing down."

Do you believe you've formed any destructive habits when it comes to your speech? How can you find out for sure?

DEADLY POISON

Can we agree there are a whole lot of scary animals in the world today? Lions and tigers and bears, oh my!

In your opinion, what's the scariest animal in the world?

Here's the thing: Every animal on land, in the sea, and in the air has the potential to be domesticated and has been tamed! Pause for a moment and take in the magnitude of that. Imagine how terrifying a lion was the first time our ancestors came across one. Now we have them do tricks in the circus! We make eight-ton elephants dress up in cute outfits. We make bears ride bicycles. Even killer whales are doing tricks for our kids!

James speaks to this:

> "For every kind of beast and bird, of reptile and sea creature, can be tamed and has been tamed by mankind, but no human being can tame the tongue. It is a restless evil, full of deadly poison" (vv. 7-8).

THIS CHANGES EVERYTHING

James knew human beings have the capacity to soften and subdue any animal that crosses our path. But he also knew we're incapable of taming our tongues. Despite everything else we've accomplished, we just can't keep our mouths shut.

Look at Proverbs 10:

> **"When words are many, transgression is not lacking,**
> **but whoever restrains his lips is prudent" (v. 19).**

Have you seen this to be true in your speech or that of others? Explain.

Which people from your circles of influence do a good job of restraining their speech? What's the practical result of that restraint?

But why must this be? Why do we have such a difficult time with our speech? James already hinted at the answer in verse 8, saying our tongue is "a restless evil, full of deadly poison." He compares our mouths to those of serpents, spewing venom that can kill. He borrows this language from the Psalmist.

> **"Deliver me, O Lord, from evil men;**
> **preserve me from violent men,**
> **who plan evil things in their heart**
> **and stir up wars continually.**
> **They make their tongue sharp as a serpent's,**
> **and under their lips is the venom of asps" (Psalm 140:1-3).**

When Paul aims to answer the question, "What are godless people like?" he quotes this same Psalm:

> **"'Their throat is an open grave;**
> **they use their tongues to deceive.'**
> **'The venom of asps is under their lips'" (Romans 3:13).**

 St. Augustine on James: "... he does not say that no one can tame the tongue, but no one of men; so that when it is tamed we confess that this is brought about by the pity, the help, the grace of God."[3]

In other words, this kind of mouth is the hallmark of those who do not know God. If you recall the purpose of James's letter, you know he has a problem with that. A relationship with God changes everything, including how we speak. This is our final point.

IT SHOULD NOT BE THIS WAY

I hope by now you've picked up on the fact that James hated duplicity. He wanted us to be consistent. He has been beating this drum all along. Don't pray to God and then doubt that He can come through (James 1:8). Don't honor Jesus and denigrate His people (James 2:1-13). Don't claim to have faith while not showing the works of faith (James 2:14-26). Be consistent!

Here James declares that it is weird to praise God and then make fun of people God made.

> **"With it we bless our Lord and Father, and with it we curse people who are made in the likeness of God" (3:9).**

Why did James emphasize that people are "made in the likeness of God"?

I've been to many a worship service where people have sung songs of praise to God, and then voiced annoyance at all manner of people in the room for all types of petty grievances. How do you think God feels about that? It is a glaring inconsistency in our behavior to praise God and mock that which He has made.

If someone came up to me and said, "Ben, I think you're the greatest. I really want you to be one of my closest friends. But I can't stand your little daughter. No offense, but I just hate her." How do you think that's going to go? There is no separation between me and my kid. One of the greatest ways you could bless me is by encouraging my daughter. One of the quickest ways to offend me is to mock her.

That's the idea James wanted to communicate. How can we use one side of our mouth to praise God and sing hymns to Him and quote psalms at Him, and then use the other side to curse His children? How can we claim He's great and then speak slanderously about the people He created in His image? Do we really think that will go over well for us?

> **"From the same mouth come blessing and cursing. My brothers, these things ought not to be so" (v. 10).**

Every moment we're alive is a gift from God. The ability to speak, form sentences, and express ideas is a gift from Him. So when we enter into a time with friends, and speak to people whom God has made with the mouth He has given us, what do we say? Do our words build up or tear down?

We who live in Christ should speak words that give life. Anything other than that is strange.

> **"Does a spring pour forth from the same opening both fresh and salt water? Can a fig tree, my brothers, bear olives, or a grapevine produce figs? Neither can a salt pond yield fresh water (vv. 11-12).**

It is absurd for one kind of thing to produce something of a totally different kind. Everything in the world produces something according to its own nature. Salt ponds produce salt water because they're salty. Fig trees produce figs because they're fig trees, while grapevines produce grapes because they're grapevines. That's the natural order of things.

In the same way, Christians should produce words that reflect and honor Christ—because we are Christians. We should produce blessings because we've been blessed. The fact that we've been given life physically, emotionally, and spiritually should naturally cause us to produce more life.

And if that's not happening, something is deeply wrong.

 In Luke 6:43-45, Jesus does not say, "produce good fruit and maybe one day you'll be a good tree." Your nature is set first (good tree) and then you naturally produce things consistent with your nature.

Think about the words you said today. Were they life-giving words?

The disturbing thing is James drops us off here! This forces us to think, *What do we do with this?* James is calling for consistency. A thing should produce that which is consistent with its nature. Where is he getting this? Again, he's drawing from the words of his brother . . .

> **"For no good tree bears bad fruit, nor again does a bad tree bear good fruit, for each tree is known by its own fruit. For figs are not gathered from thornbushes, nor are grapes picked from a bramble bush. The good person out of the good treasure of his heart produces good, and the evil person out of his evil treasure produces evil, for out of the abundance of the heart his mouth speaks" (Luke 6:43-45).**

How would you summarize Jesus' teaching in these verses?

According to Jesus, people who have evil hearts produce an abundance of evil stuff from their mouths—from the way they speak. But people with good hearts produce an abundance of good fruit from their mouths. So if Jesus were to give advice on how to stop our destructive speech, He wouldn't tell us to watch our mouths; He would tell us to watch our hearts.

That's the same advice we heard from James. He said trees automatically produce fruit according to their natures. So it doesn't make sense to work hard at producing good fruit and hope you'll become a good tree one day. No, when God makes you a good tree, you'll naturally produce good fruit.

 For more on producing "good fruit,"
compare Matthew 7:15-20; 15:1-2,16-20;
Luke 6:43-45; John 4:13-14; 7:37-39.

What we need is not a list of tips on how to control our mouths. We need the grace of God to course mightily through our hearts. Jesus said in John 7,

> **"On the last day of the feast, the great day, Jesus stood up and cried out, 'If anyone thirsts, let him come to me and drink. Whoever believes in me, as the Scripture has said, "Out of his heart will flow rivers of living water."' Now this he said about the Spirit, whom those who believed in him were to receive, for as yet the Spirit had not been given, because Jesus was not yet glorified" (John 7:37-39).**

When God blesses you with living water, the springs of your heart will overflow with clean water.

How do you react to the above statements? Why?

Now let me ask this question: What would happen if we discovered that our emptiness has already been filled? What would happen if we figured out that we are already OK? What if we realized that we're already loved, treasured, appreciated, and fulfilled? We wouldn't have to defend ourselves anymore. We wouldn't have to try to build ourselves up by cutting others down.

So that's my advice to you—that's James's advice to you and Jesus' advice to you. Turn your heart toward your Father and say: "God, I'm tempted to tell people how awesome I am because I feel like I need their approval to make me OK. Lord, would You help me see that You are my Dad because of grace? Help me see that I'm already OK."

And when you feel that hellfire start to burn between your lips, say: "God, I want to mock this person to vindicate myself and prove some point, but I don't need to do that. God, I can trust You."

As you realize your Father is the One taking care of you, I promise you'll understand that things really are going to be OK. And that kind of realization will begin to change how you speak for the rest of your life.

APPLY TO LIFE

> **PRAY:** Take time to pray this week, asking God to help you focus on the reasons why we say terrible things. Pray for strength and guidance to build others up with your words far more than you tear them down.

> **REFLECT:** What would change in our world if we always spoke the truth in love? How would the world be different if we always showed respect to people because they're in the image of God?

> **STUDY:** Try this experiment: The next time you step into a classroom, your office, or your normal social circle, resolve to say nothing negative whatsoever. See if you can make it through an entire conversation. Most of our conversations are built on negativity: "Can you believe how cold/hot/rainy it is?" "I am so tired." "I am so stressed." "I can't believe we have to do this." Try to respond positively to everything; I promise you'll sound like a weirdo—but in a good way. We have so habituated negativity that we can't make it through an entire conversation without it.

> **LISTEN:** Purchase "Speak Life" by tobyMac and "Words" by Hawk Nelson from the *This Changes Everything* playlist. Add these to your regular mix of music this week to be reminded of the power of your words.

NOTES

IF THE LORD WILLS

> "Come now, you who say, 'Today or tomorrow we will go into such and such a town and spend a year there and trade and make a profit'—yet you do not know what tomorrow will bring. What is your life? For you are a mist that appears for a little time and then vanishes. Instead you ought to say, 'If the Lord wills, we will live and do this or that.' As it is, you boast in your arrogance. All such boasting is evil. So whoever knows the right thing to do and fails to do it, for him it is sin."
>
> James 4:13-17

A few years ago my wife, Donna, and I spent the summer speaking to youth camps all over the United States. Toward the end of our last camp, we decided to stop by a Starbucks® one morning to have a devotional time before jumping back into camp life. While we were there a young man snatched my wife's iPhone® right off the table in front of us—actually ripped her earbuds out—and took off toward the door. This was a fascinating moment because you always wonder, *What would I do in that situation? What would my instinctual reaction be?*

My wife's first reaction was to shout, "Get 'em babe!" In that moment, what are you going to do? Say, "no thank you"? So I kicked my flip-flops off and chased him. We turned the corner, and I instantly spotted a security car and began to call for help—that is until I discovered that his buddy was sitting behind the wheel. It was their get-away car. Then, all in a moment, he jumped in the car, I grabbed the door, and his friend hit the gas. So for several minutes we drove down the street—them in the vehicle and me hanging from the passenger side door. This was interesting, given that we actually had a conversation while driving. They were young, the same age as the kids I had been preaching to all week, so I was talking softly to them. They were calling me "sir." It was strange. But, in the end, I realized I had two options: jump in the car with them or let go because this hanging-from-the-side deal was getting old. I decided to let go.

That night my back began to hurt. Then it hurt a little more the next day. And on the third day I woke up in significant pain. I wasn't able to stand. Waves of pain shot down my left leg and its strength declined.

We met with several doctors. Each time I told them my schedule and the things I had planned to do that week. I explained that I didn't have time for this, and therefore, I needed them to hurry up and fix it.

Finally one surgeon put it to me as straight as he could: I had three herniated discs in my lower back. Because of my previous back injuries, any surgical option would run the risk of destabilizing my spine in the future. He informed me that I had to cancel all my speaking engagements. I would have to find someone else to do my job at Breakaway. More than that, he expressed doubt that I would be able to hold our baby girl, who was due in just a couple of months. He also voiced concern that I could lose the use of my left leg.

So a simple trip to Starbucks turned into a month of me being pumped full of drugs and lying on my face on the floor of my living room. All my plans crumbled like a house of cards due to this unforeseen incident. Suddenly I realized with unwavering clarity: I don't have nearly as much control over my life as I thought I did just a few short days ago.

Have you experienced anything that immediately affected your view over the control of your life? Explain.

Watch the *This Changes Everything* video for Session 6, available at *threadsmedia.com/thischangeseverything*.

THE BEST LAID PLANS . . .

> "Come now, you who say, 'Today or tomorrow we will go into such and such a town and spend a year there and trade and make a profit'" (James 4:13).

James begins this section with the confrontational exclamation, "Come now!" It's like saying, "Hey! Listen up!" James aims to grab the collar of a certain group of people. They appear to be Christian businessmen. He wrote the letter to believers in Jesus, and he speaks of these particular members of the community traveling to make money. Yet before those of us who aren't Christian business people dismiss this section, notice that the language is broad enough to encompass a wider circle. In reality, James confronts anyone who might say the following things:

1. I plan on traveling somewhere.
2. I plan on arriving someplace.
3. I plan on spending a certain amount of time there.
4. I plan on doing something when I get there.
5. I plan for that activity to have a certain outcome.

So if you've ever planned to go somewhere, do something, and expect a certain result, James wants to have a word with you. If you've said something like, "I am going to college to get a degree," then James has a problem with you. If you have ever said something like, "I want to move to Los Angeles and be a schoolteacher," James will call you arrogant. If you have said, "I think I'm going to Austin this weekend," James calls you *evil!*

What's his problem? Does James believe it's wrong to plan? Does he think it's wrong to make a profit or expect success? No. (As we'll see in verse 15, he showed us a legitimate way to plan to do something.)

Then what is his issue with these people? Their failure is not in *what* they rise up to do, but in *how they talk* about doing the things they do. And it's not just about words. It's about *perspective*. The problem: These people have the wrong perspective. They have a distorted picture of (1) life and (2) God—and it affects their plans. Verse 14 speaks to the true view of life that's not being taken into account when they plan. Verse 15 addresses the true view of God that is not being taken into account when they plan. Let's take them one at a time.

A CORRECT PERSPECTIVE ON LIFE

> "Yet you do not know what tomorrow will bring. What is your life? For you are a mist that appears for a little time and then vanishes" (v. 14).

What realities about life does James present in this verse?

How does it make you feel to hear your life compared to a mist? How might that impact your planning?

James first corrects the failure to see ourselves rightly. He identifies two errors in our perspective on life.

1. We do not know the content of tomorrow.
That is true of all of us. We are limited. We have no idea what tomorrow may bring. We may meet "the One" and get married. We may get hit by a bus. We can make plans, but reality never shifts to conform to our expectations. This should engender a little humility. We don't run this place. So we may make our plans, but we err if we assume that means they will happen.

In what ways do you assume that you know what tomorrow will bring?

Have there been instances where life surprised you? Explain a few.

While this insight into our lack of foresight bears considerable attention, it is not James's main point in this verse. In fact, verses 13-14 are all one sentence in the original language and all of it builds to the next point.

James calls readers not simply to contemplate their lack of knowledge of the future, but to pull back the lens and assess the very nature of existence. *What kind of life do you have, exactly? What is its quality?* Before we can answer, James will tell us explicitly:

> **"For you are a mist that appears for a little time and then vanishes"**
> **(v. 14).**

2. We fail to appreciate the fragility of human life. We are not here long.
This is the second failure of those of us who plan so cavalierly. James calls us smoke that dances into the light for the briefest of moments, then vanishes. James wants us to grasp and appreciate the reality that there's nothing of enduring substance about us. There is a fragility to human life.

We don't like to hear this. In fact, we lose this perspective all the time. We can get so locked in on achieving a particular goal that we lose sight of the reality that we possess a very limited amount of time here. But proof of this reality surrounds us.

Cast your mind back to 10 years ago. What was the most amazing thing you owned? What were you obsessed with acquiring? What was popular? Does it matter at all now? Find a picture of what you were wearing 10 years ago. Back then you thought it looked awesome. How does it appear now?

Ten years is not a very long time in the grand scheme. Yet look at what has happened to you. Some of you were playing on a jungle gym at recess 10 years ago.

Now you're in college. Some of you were in college 10 years ago. Now you're losing your hair and wondering why your back hurts all the time.

What is happening to you? It's called life. It moves quickly. We fade fast. We are "a mist."

Now what bearing does this have on our propensity to plan? Does this mean we should stop planning? No. But it should inform our planning. Knowing that we don't last long helps us prioritize. What truly matters?

If you're here just to race to get a degree to get a job to make some money to buy a house to raise some kids so they can get a good education so they can get a job to make some money to buy a house to raise some kids so they can get a good education . . . you need to stop and ask yourself what all of that is for.

What have you been focused on that won't have meaning in 10 years?

We tend to put down our heads and fixate on whatever is in front of us. James calls us to pick up our heads and see the big picture. We are going to die. This inescapable reality should inform how we live.

Jonathan Edwards, arguably the greatest thinker America has ever produced, wrote this in his journal as a young man: "Resolved, to think much on all occasions of my own dying, and of the common circumstances which attend death."[1] You may read that and think, *Wow. Sounds like a morbid guy.* But I dare say he was more in touch with reality than we are. The Puritans used to place their cemeteries in the center of town. These served as reminders as they conducted the business of the day: *This day is a gift. One of these days I will be there.*

Let me ask you a question: Where is the closest cemetery to your home? Do you even know? Many of us do not. We hide them in America today. We can point out the closest mall in a heartbeat. Cemeteries? We don't think about those. But we are all headed there. Why would I want you to think about this?

Moses wrote this in reference to humanity:

> "They are like grass that grows in the morning—
> in the morning it sprouts and grows;
> by evening it withers and dries up. . . .
> Teach us to number our days carefully
> so that we may develop wisdom in our hearts"
> (Psalm 90:5b-6,12, HCSB).

Biblically, we realize it's a good thing to consider the fact that we're going to die because it will affect how we live!

In Luke 12:18, Jesus told the story of a man who experienced great success in agriculture and found himself with a surplus of goods. In the midst of this abundance, he made a decision to store his wealth, retire, and enjoy life for years to come. Jesus then offered His assessment of that logic: foolish. Jesus declared that the man was destined to die that very night, and he had failed to be rich toward God. The man intended to use his wealth to buy comforts, assuming he had years to live like this. Yet in reality, only two things in existence are eternal: God and human beings. It would have been much better to invest wealth in caring for people, whom God loves, than in spending it on the latest luxury item. Knowledge of the brevity of life should lead us to live a better quality life.

Don't get caught with your head down thinking only about stuff that truly will not matter in a year. Lift your eyes today and value what matters. Enjoy the sunrise. Share your meals with friends. Show kindness to strangers. Live a life that truly matters.

If you knew you were going to die tomorrow, what would you do today?

Why are you not doing those things now?

If we ended the session now, then this wouldn't be a distinctively Christian message. We could have watched the movie *The Bucket List* or listened to the song "I Hope You Dance" and received the same advice. Yet James did not end his argument here. Failing to appreciate the transient nature of our lives is only the first mistake. There is a second, far more costly mistake.

SEE GOD . . .

James identifies the second failure in perspective in verse 15:

> **"Instead you ought to say, 'If the Lord wills, we will live and do this or that.'"**

Why does James use the word "instead"? To what does it refer earlier in the Scripture passage?

James's use of "instead" connects two verses: "Come now, you who say" (v. 13), *and* "Instead you ought to say" (v. 15).

James urges us to add a key qualifier to our planning: "If the Lord wills." Now some may be tempted to roll their eyes at James. *This is what he's after? He wants us to add "If the Lord wills" to every sentence before we say it? Seems silly.* Yet before you dismiss James as a legalist, understand that this is not simply a statement about semantics. Jesus said "out of the abundance of the heart his mouth speaks" (Luke 6:45). James does not simply want us to alter our words. He wants a new perspective to sink deep into our hearts and inform every word we speak.

So what is the second mistake the planners in verse 13 made? They failed to see God rightly. It's not enough to have a correct view of ourselves in mind as we make plans. We must also have a proper view of God as we make plans. So what is the proper view?

James listed two important things about God in verse 15. What are these identifiers?

IF THE LORD WILLS, WE WILL LIVE

The first thing James wants us to understand about God is just that: "If the Lord wills, we will live . . ." It is not enough to understand that our lives are short. We must go further and understand that God determines how long we live.

The apostle Paul understood this. In Acts 18:21 he left Ephesus and said, "I will return to you if God wills." In 1 Corinthians 4:19 he wrote, "I will come to you soon, if the Lord wills." Paul faced threats in almost every city he entered. He never knew which day was his last. Yet he acknowledged that his end would be determined by no one else but the Lord.

Have you had someone you know face the possibility of his or her imminent death? Describe that situation.

How did this situation inform his or her view of life? How did it affect his or her view of God?

We do not control whether we live or die. He does. This reality should produce in us a deep sense of humility. We continue to exist today solely because of His grace. This truth will also bring either a sense of fear or a sense of comfort, depending on how well you know Him who rules life and death.

IF THE LORD WILLS, WE WILL DO THIS OR THAT

The second thing James wants us to understand about God is the remainder of verse 15:

> **"If the Lord wills, we will live and do this or that."**

God not only ordains the end of our lives; He determines what we accomplish with our lives!

When I first took over as director of Breakaway Ministries, I was excited about the possibilities. Already there were thousands of students coming. I could not wait to dive into the role of shepherd of this amazing ministry. Then I took a look at our financial statements.

On my first day, I discovered that we had more bills than income. I called a member of the Board of Directors for perspective. He confirmed my fears: These were the worst financial numbers the ministry had ever seen. I got the sinking feeling that I had just signed on to be the captain of the Titanic.

After a brief moment of panic, I did the only thing I could do: I called the team together to pray. We had no other recourse than to throw ourselves at the mercy of God. That month we received the largest amount of donations we had ever received. We paid our bills and continued to sail on. Yet our perspective had totally changed. Now when people ask me what it's like leading such an incredible ministry, I answer, *I am so grateful that the Lord allows me to do this.* Those are more than just words. I believe God put me through that moment of crisis during my first week in the office to help me understand what had always been true: God determines what we get to do.

God runs all of it. You have what you have because of Him, and He determines what you will do. Dismissing Him as we live the life He gave us makes us out of step with reality. Not only that, it displays a serious heart problem.

"As it is, you boast in your arrogance. All such boasting is evil"
(v. 16).

Don't miss this. All verse 13 said at the beginning was, "We will go into such and such a town and . . . make a profit." James calls this "boast[ing] in your arrogance." Why? Because it is arrogant to live the life God has given us, and then with the mouth He's given us dismiss the reality that He rules every aspect of our lives. Not only is it arrogant, it is evil. It's not good for the people God made to make the mistake of thinking we can do all of this without acknowledging Him.

FOLLOWING THE LEADER

In his book *The Faith of the American Soldier,* Stephen Mansfield includes a story about Lance Corporal Darrin McKay:

> "Thickly muscled and plastered with tattoos, McKay is a smaller, meaner-looking version of Arnold Schwarzenegger. . . . His credo adorns his left arm: 'Though I walk through the valley of the shadow of death, I shall fear no evil, for I am the baddest warrior in the valley.'
>
> McKay tells everyone who will listen that he is in Iraq because 'when the going gets tough, the tough go Marine.' He joined up after high school in Los Angeles because he wanted to experience, '*Fear Factor* on stun,' a reference to the popular television show in which contestants confront their fears to win prizes. . . . He is here to prove himself and to return home as 'bad as any mother's son who ever walked the earth.'"[2]

The book goes on to tell of McKay's closest friend, "Dogman," who was killed in battle next to McKay. After experiencing the horrific event, McKay is forever changed:

"It is a week later now. . . . Death, which has always seemed at bay from his strong, arrogant life, is now as close as his breath. He will end; someday, somehow, he will end. . . . Death is asking Darrin McKay who he is and what he believes. But he does not know. 'Dogman was the best of us,' McKay says quietly, refusing a tear, 'and he went in an instant. I probably will too. But I wish I knew something about what's on the other side. I wish I believed something or I had done something that makes it all worthwhile. I hate the thought of dying, but I hate the thought of dying empty most of all.'"[3]

As we close, we need to ask one more important question: How can this be good news? The thought of death's inevitable embrace does not fill most people with joy and confidence. The fact that someone else controls our fate can be disconcerting as well. How are we supposed to feel good about this? Fortunately, James's word choice helps us here.

The phrase, "if the gods will," was common in the Greek culture of James's day. That was not a distinctively Christian sentiment. For the Greeks that statement was said with a bit of resignation: *We are subject to the whims of fickle gods. What can we do?* Notice James did not say it that way. James identified the Lord in verse 1 of his letter, "the Lord Jesus Christ," and recognized His authority over all. Why is this significant? Because whether we chafe under leadership or rejoice under it, it's directly related to who is doing the leading!

Stephen Ambrose's bestselling book *Band of Brothers* chronicles the exploits of the men of the 101st airborne during World War II. After the Battle of Bastogne, the men were charged with taking the city of Foy away from Nazi forces. Unfortunately, at the time the company was under the command of Lieutenant Dike. The men believed he was self-serving and indecisive—terrifying characteristics to see in the leader who controls your fate. While attempting to take the city, Lieutenant Dike panicked and made the men pause the attack at the most vulnerable moment. As he folded under pressure, his superior officers replaced him with another leader, Lieutenant Speirs. The men then watched as Speirs charged into the field to unite with them and lead them into the city.

The enemy fired their largest guns at him to no avail. When the men of the 101st saw this man risk his life without hesitation for their sake, they were impressed. The morale shifted instantly. Where fear had hampered them, now they were filled with courage. Why? They were willing to follow joyfully the man they knew would risk his life on their behalf.[4]

When have you seen leadership stifle or strengthen people?

What makes a good leader? Who can you name that embodies these qualities?

THE ULTIMATE EXAMPLE

We know the character of the man who directs our lives, Jesus Christ. He set His face like stone toward Jerusalem and marched into the very jaws of death for us. He faced down sin, death, and hell for us. He did this not only at the risk of His life but at the *cost* of His life. And He beat death, that whoever trusts in Him might have life. This is the Lord who guides our future. When we know that the one leading us loves us like this, we can smile at the days to come. We can joyfully submit to His will in this life. We can easily obey His commands on how to handle money, how to use our sexuality, or how to treat the poor, because we know His ways are best. We can embrace His intended trajectory for our lives. No longer do we use this life to chase things that will fade, but we can focus on what truly matters.

How can the fact that the Lord rules our lives be an encouraging thought to us?

A CHANGE IN PERSPECTIVE

After a month of lying on my back, the pain began to decrease. Strength began to return to my leg, and I was able to walk into my surgeon's office. He was shocked. Though not a Christian, he exclaimed, "Someone up there must like you, because I can't believe that you're walking."

I do believe that Someone up there likes me, but not because He gave me back the ability to walk, though I am grateful! He gave me something even more amazing during that month on the floor. Without realizing it, I had started to care too much about things that did not really matter: my reputation, my success, and so forth. I had falsely believed I could plan out my days. I had begun to care less about the things that truly do matter: loving God and loving people. I now believe God put me on my back for this very reason, to return me to my senses. I don't want to waste a moment of my life obsessing about things that do not ultimately matter. Rather, I want to spend every second following my great King who gave His life for me, and join Him in loving others for His glory and their good. And, if He wills, may we all live like this together!

APPLY TO LIFE

> REFLECT: In what ways does your view of God need to shift in order to trust Him to lead your life?

> STUDY: Visit *desiringGod.org* and search for "The Resolutions of Jonathan Edwards." Read and reflect on all of them. Print them out and tape them to your wall or put them beside your bed. Commit to read over the list every day for two weeks. Journal through the process.

> LISTEN: Purchase "Nothing Is Wasted" by Elevation Worship and "Ruin Me" by Jeff Johnson from the *This Changes Everything* playlist. Add these to your regular mix of music this week to focus on God's will.

NOTES

GOD, MONEY AND THE LAS DAYS

> "Be patient, therefore, brothers, until the coming of the Lord. See how the farmer waits for the precious fruit of the earth, being patient about it, until it receives the early and the late rains. You also, be patient. Establish your hearts, for the coming of the Lord is at hand. Do not grumble against one another, brothers, so that you may not be judged; behold, the Judge is standing at the door. As an example of suffering and patience, brothers, take the prophets who spoke in the name of the Lord. Behold, we consider those blessed who remained steadfast. You have heard of the steadfastness of Job, and you have seen the purpose of the Lord, how the Lord is compassionate and merciful."
>
> James 5:7-11

I remember when The Notorious B.I.G.'s record *Life After Death* released. That summer the hit single "Mo Money Mo Problems" played incessantly. In the song, Puff Daddy (as he was known at the time), Mase, and B.I.G. lamented about having more problems the more money they made. I'll be honest—it was hard to sympathize. Most people I knew would gladly exchange their problems for the issues that come with having too much money. Maybe, that is, until they read this passage in James. Perhaps Biggie was more prophetic than he realized.

James 5:1-12 is a rough text. The Book of James as a whole is tough; he has called us "adulteresses" and "demonic," and now he goes after the rich. However, James was not the first to speak about the rich in this harsh way. He's following a thread we see all throughout Scripture, but the thread is not simply a consistent curse on the rich. The common thread is God's care for people.

The Pentateuch, the first five books of the Bible, tells the story of God choosing to set His affections on a group of people, the Israelites, whom He snatched out of slavery in Egypt and formed into a mighty nation. God gave His Law to His people and taught them how to live as a community.

He intended for them to be a shining beacon of light, displaying His glory for the world to see.

Part of God's plan all along was not simply to rescue the Israelites out of bondage but also to bless them. He promised them bread and wine, flocks and herds, and a land flowing with milk and honey. But with God's blessings came these commands:

> **"When you reap the harvest of your land, you shall not reap your field right up to its edge, neither shall you gather the gleanings after your harvest. And you shall not strip your vineyard bare, neither shall you gather the fallen grapes of your vineyard. You shall leave them for the poor and for the sojourner: I am the LORD your God" (Leviticus 19:9-10).**

What was God's command to the Israelites?

When God blessed His people with prosperity, He made it clear that their good fortunes were not just for them. They were to leave their excess grain and fruit for others in the community who needed it—for those who were sick, poor, or in need in some way. If the Israelites thought back to the days when they were in bondage, they would remember that they once had nothing, and God blessed them with bread, flocks, land, and so forth. As God's people, they were to use His generosity to them to bless others.

The Israelites failed to model God's character in this way. Later in their history, they grew prosperous and greedy, and it became common for rich land-owners to exploit their hired workers. As a result, in Proverbs, "rich" can occasionally be used as a synonym for "unrighteous." God was unhappy, not with the fact that His people were blessed with riches, but because they chose to hoard their wealth and take advantage of those who had less.

 Compare Leviticus 19:9-10 with how God cares for the "foreigner, the fatherless, and the widow" in Deuteronomy 14:29; 26:12.

THIS CHANGES EVERYTHING

The prophets voiced God's anger in passages such as Jeremiah 22:

> "Woe to him who builds his house by unrighteousness,
>   and his upper rooms by injustice,
> who makes his neighbor serve him for nothing
>   and does not give him his wages,
> who says, 'I will build myself a great house
>   with spacious upper rooms,'
> who cuts out windows for it,
>   paneling it with cedar
>   and painting it with vermilion.
> Do you think you are a king
>   because you compete in cedar?
> Did not your father eat and drink
>   and do justice and righteousness?
>   Then it was well with him.
> He judged the cause of the poor and needy;
>   then it was well.
> Is not this to know me?
>   declares the LORD.
> But you have eyes and heart
>   only for your dishonest gain,
> for shedding innocent blood,
>   and for practicing oppression and violence" (vv. 13-17).

Describe what's happening in these verses in your own words.

What parallel situation in our own time and culture can you think of?

What's God's response to the way His people misuse and oppress the poor?

Watch the *This Changes Everything* video for Session 7, available at *threadsmedia.com/thischangeseverything.*

God is angry because His people are not valuing what He values. For this, He will bring judgment.

Back when I was a youth pastor, I led a bunch of our students on a whitewater rafting trip. I did not lead the actual rafting part, of course; we hired several guides whose job was to take groups of students down the river.

One guide was particularly goofy. He kept messing around and showing off. Everyone was laughing and having a good time—right up until the moment that guide took his raft, carrying eight or more kids, and rammed it into a bridge. The raft split open and sent all the kids tumbling into the frigid water.

Thankfully, everyone was OK. (Life jackets come in handy, right?) I remember getting back on the bus and observing that guide. The other rafting guides were attempting to joke with him: "Ha ha, that was funny how you ruined that thousand-dollar raft and almost killed everybody." But the guy was not responding to any of it. He was hunched over and looked like he might vomit or start crying, or both.

I tapped one of the other guides on the shoulder and asked what was wrong with him. She answered, "You want to know why he looks so scared? We only have one rule in this job: Protect the raft and the people on it. That guy broke our only rule because he was messing around, trying to be cool. He will have to face the owner of the company once we get back to headquarters, and he knows he's not only going to be fired, but held responsible for the cost of the raft."

In other words, there was one rule and that guy did not keep it. The boss valued one thing and he failed to value it. For that reason, judgment was coming. This is exactly what James is saying.

> **"Come now, you rich, weep and howl for the miseries that are coming upon you. Your riches have rotted and your garments are moth-eaten. Your gold and silver have corroded, and their corrosion will be evidence against you and will eat your flesh like fire. You have laid up treasure in the last days"** (James 5:1-3).

UNDERSTANDING "WEALTH"

Like the prophets, James calls the wealthy to "weep and howl" (v. 1). Not only cry, but wail! Why? Because miseries are coming upon them. A day of slaughter is coming, and there's evidence that will convict them.

He tells the rich that their material possessions will not last. Notice he puts the verbs in past tense: It's so certain they will fade that James speaks as if it has already happened. Yet this is not the worst part. The corrosion of their goods will serve as evidence against them!

James paints the picture of a courtroom. As they stand on trial, the damning evidence against them will be a big pile of their corroded wealth.

Why does he say that? Is it wrong to have money? No. The problem is in verse 3: "You have laid up treasure in the last days." Why should the rich cry? Because they hoarded money. They were selfish with their wealth.

So is the Bible against saving? No! The Bible actually commends saving as wise. Read Proverbs 6.

> **"Go to the ant, O sluggard;**
> **consider her ways, and be wise.**
> **Without having any chief,**
> **officer, or ruler,**
> **she prepares her bread in summer**
> **and gathers her food in harvest" (vv. 6-8).**

Hoarding, however, is a different matter. The Bible is clearly anti-hoarding. Stockpiling wealth simply for ourselves contradicts God's plan for society. God has blessed us, and we're meant to use those resources to bless other people. If we make our gifts all about us, we distort God's intention in blessing us, and God will deal with us. The rich in this passage should be terrified because they did not play the game right. God cares about people, and we are supposed to leverage our wealth, which will fade, to bless others.

What also makes this atrocious is that James' audience was hoarding "in the last days." What does James mean by "the last days"? Well, history follows a timeline. It began with creation, when God made everything, including human beings. Then there was the fall, when sin entered the world. But not long after this fall, God made a promise to rescue; He sent Jesus, who brought redemption to humanity. Jesus died on the cross, taking the penalty for our sins, and then He rose again victorious over sin and death. After His resurrection, He ascended into heaven, but He told His disciples that He was coming back. And the period between His ascension into heaven and the moment He returns is known as the "last days." James lived in these days and so do we. All that remains on the eschatological calendar is the return of the King. And when He returns, He wants to see us reflecting His values. And here James tells us that this day of His return is not a secret. And the rich knew this day was coming.

The brevity of time before His arrival should affect how we play the game.

I remember the first time I played the Madden NFL® video game. I was playing against a buddy of mine, and I was terrible. My defense could not stop him from scoring points, and my offense was failing to run any quality plays. He was crushing me.

But then all of a sudden I started making some headway by running the ball straight up the middle. I would hand the ball to my running back and have him plow forward for five yards, seven yards, four yards, and it was working. I was driving down the field. I was going to score!

And then the game just stopped. Nothing was working. I looked over at my buddy and said, "What's wrong with your game?"

He looked back at me and said, "You're an idiot. The game stopped because the time has run out. The game is over. It was the fourth quarter with two minutes left to play, and you kept sending out those stupid running plays up the middle. Why didn't you try to pass and score a touchdown?"

I didn't have a comeback. It had never crossed my mind to check and see how much time was left.

According to James, the same thing was true of the rich people in his day. They were hoarding wealth and not paying attention to the clock in "the last days." God's assessment: you have money. I value people; therefore, you should have spent that money to care for people. And when the clock ran out, you were sitting on a pile of money while the world was full of hurting people. I have a serious problem with that.

Again, God does not have a problem with people prospering financially. What he has a problem with is devaluing people. Here James highlights a terrible principle: The more you love money, the less you love people. Rather than using money to bless people, we use people to get more money for ourselves. This is what James condemns.

> "Behold, the wages of the laborers who mowed your fields, which you kept back by fraud, are crying out against you, and the cries of the harvesters have reached the ears of the Lord of hosts. You have lived on the earth in luxury and in self-indulgence. You have fattened your hearts in a day of slaughter. You have condemned and murdered the righteous person. He does not resist you" (vv. 4-6).

Now you may not have cheated any harvesters out of their wages lately, but we can so easily slip into this mode of thinking where we care more about our comfort than we do about God's children.

In Rousseau's autobiographical work *Confessions,* written in 1770, he tells of a "thoughtless saying of a great princess, who, on being informed that the country people had no bread, replied, 'Then let them eat pastry!'"[1] Her complete obliviousness to the plight of the poor is horrifying. Unfortunately, we're not as far from her as we would like to think.

Slaveryfootprint.org, a website designed to help people discover their connection to modern-day slavery, asks a few seemingly innocent questions concerning the clothes I buy, the food I eat, and the electronics I own. I dutifully type them in, and I'm then horrified by the result: I have 63 slaves working for me. There are more slaves today than any other time in human history, and many of them make the products I use every day. God does not like this.

In 2012, the Generosity Index in the United States crunched numbers about the country's most generous states. Ironically, some of the country's poorest states also contain some of the country's most charitable people. Four of the poorest states made the top 10 list of most charitable by average donation amount *and* percentage of salary, while only one of the top 10 states found on the "richest states" list made it onto the top 10 in charitable giving.[2]

What does this tell us? As in James's day, so it is today. The harvesters are being abused, and the rich are not generous. The more we love money, the less we value people. And God hates this.

James declares that their cries have reached the ears of "the Lord of hosts." Notice he does not call Him "Daddy God" or "sweet, tender Jesus." He points to God's role as the Commander-in-Chief of His angel armies. The God of the mightiest army in existence is coming to judge the world, and those who have lived in luxury and self-indulgence have fattened themselves up for that day of slaughter. His language is meant to unnerve us.

Does this make you feel uncomfortable? Why or why not?

We should feel uncomfortable. But let's turn the corner and ask the most important question we can at this moment: Should we run from money? How do we avoid being numbered among those fattened for the day of slaughter?

JESUS AND MONEY

In Luke 12 Jesus warns His disciples:

> "Take care, and be on your guard against all covetousness, for one's life does not consist in the abundance of his possessions" (v. 15).

Then, in Luke 12:13-21, Jesus tells the parable of the rich man who, upon enjoying a bountiful harvest, makes the decision to hoard it for a luxurious retirement. Jesus' assessment: the man is a fool, for he was appointed to die that night, and he had failed to be rich toward God.

Jesus implored His disciples to seek the Father's kingdom, and God would provide for them. He told them to sell their possessions and give to the poor, and thus have treasure in heaven, which cannot fade. He concludes by telling them:

> "For where your treasure is, there will your heart be also" (Luke 12:34).

Money isn't really the issue. It's our hearts. Do we care about people, or do we care about possessions? Do we love others, or do we love ourselves? Money just reveals what's happening in our hearts.

Money is like a knife. Is a knife a weapon? Maybe. It depends on who is wielding it. A knife in the hands of a murderer is a terrifying thing. It can take a life. But a knife in the hand of a surgeon is a beautiful thing. It can save a life. What matters is the heart of the person using it. Money is like this. It can be something you hoard and use to exploit others, or it is something you can use to encourage others.

When looking at your life, how do you use money?

List a few practical ways this week that you can bless others with what God has given you.

If we use money for self-indulgence, then we are cross-purposes with God, and we have reason to fear His day of arrival. Yet this is not the only option.

THE LAST DAYS

James switches gears and audiences:

> **"Be patient, therefore, brothers, until the coming of the Lord. See how the farmer waits for the precious fruit of the earth, being patient about it, until it receives the early and the late rains. You also, be patient. Establish your hearts, for the coming of the Lord is at hand" (James 5:7-8).**

He commanded the rich to be afraid, for the end of days meant judgment.

Here James tells the "brothers" (i.e. Christians) to be patient like a farmer, until the day of the Lord comes. What does that mean? A farmer works hard for months, but for a long while, when he looks out across his field, all he sees is dirt. He must wait patiently for the day of harvest. And when it comes, there is celebration.

Do you see the contrast?

For the rich, there is comfort now, but they should be terrified of the day of the Lord. For the brothers there is dirt and hard work now, but they should be encouraged by the day of the Lord. It is not a day of judgment. It is a day of reaping a harvest and celebrating.

The coming of the Lord can either be a scary thing or an exciting thing.

How does the coming of the Lord affect the way you live each day and how you view your current situation in life?

If you recall the story of Robin Hood, the action takes place in England while the king is away. In the king's absence, two parties emerge. Some, led by the sheriff, live in palaces and hoard money by exploiting the people. Others, led by Robin Hood, live in a forest and give money away to the poor. One hoards selfishly. One gives generously. Then, the king returns! Those who had taken advantage of his subjects for their own luxury are terrified. While those who had maintained their allegiance to the king rejoice at his return. Whether you are mourning or rejoicing in that day has everything to do with whether or not you lived a life that reflected the values of the king. The same is true for us.

You don't need to know Greek to understand the New Testament, but there's a word that, when the Lord comes back, all the believers from the first century will be yelling and I just want you to know what they are saying. The word is *parousia*. *Ousia* means "exist" or "be present." *Para* means "with" or "alongside." To the Greeks the word was often used to refer to the arrival of a king or dignitary in their city. They would hear that the king was coming. He would soon be here with us! That would often prompt them to hurry to clean the city and repair the roads so that they would be ready for the *parousia* of the king!

This is the word James uses twice in this section to refer to the "coming" of the Lord. There is a day when He will arrive in our midst! This will be terrifying to some, but it will be exciting for others. That will all depend on what we're doing when He arrives.

I want you to be happy on that day, so I want you to be about the business of the King today. What does that mean? It means I want you to leverage your money, which will fade, to bless people, whom God cares for infinitely. So get an education. Get a job. Make money. But then live generously.

Some will ask, "So how much am I supposed to give?" The New Testament does not aim at a percentage. It aims at a disposition. I want you to have a bent toward generosity. I want you to leverage your income as much as you can for the benefit of others.

When John Wesley was a student at Oxford, he arrived one day at his dormitory with a stack of pictures he had bought to decorate his room. At the moment he arrived he saw the chambermaid who, on a cold winter day, had no coat. She could not afford one. Wesley gave her some money, but it was not enough for a coat. He had spent the majority of his cash on wall decorations. This contrast bothered him. Wesley then began to control his expenses so he could have money to give to the poor. So the first year he worked he made an income of 30 pounds. He found he could live on 28, so he gave 2. The following year his income increased to 60 pounds. He lived on 28 and gave 32. By the time he was making 120 pounds, Wesley was living on 28 pounds and giving 92. That means he was giving away more than 75 percent of his income. What's the lesson? As our wealth increases, what should always rise first is not our standard of living, but our standard of giving. Decide now to be a person who lives with a bent toward generosity. I promise it's a more satisfying life.

What plan could you put in place to live generously as your wealth exceeds your cost of living?

What habits could you develop now that will make it natural to give more as you receive more from the Lord?

Not long ago at Breakaway, our ministry on the campus of Texas A&M, we put a challenge in front of our college students. An incredible ministry, Tiny Hands International, was attempting to gather funding to build homes in Nepal for young girls rescued from the brutal sex trade in India. The cost of the homes:

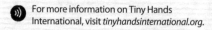 For more information on Tiny Hands International, visit *tinyhandsinternational.org*.

THIS CHANGES EVERYTHING

$42,000 each. We asked our students to give enough money to build two. Now keep in mind, these are college students. We're not talking about the wealthiest demographic in our country. But we read Jesus' words from Luke 12:33 together:

> **"Sell your possessions, and give to the needy. Provide yourselves with moneybags that do not grow old, with a treasure in the heavens that does not fail, where no thief approaches and no moth destroys."**

To be honest, I wasn't sure how our students would respond. I certainly was not prepared for what we saw happen.

Stories poured in of students selling their bicycles, video game consoles, or excess clothing and furniture. They went back to their organizations and held fund-raisers. One afternoon members of the track team at Texas A&M came literally running to the office to drop off money for these kids.

The goal by the end of one month was $84,000, but we raised $120,000. I will never forget the moment I stood on stage and told our students what they had done on behalf of these young girls. The room erupted. Loud cheers filled the arena. They were high-fiving and hugging people they didn't even know! Why? What was happening in that room? They were discovering a principle that God has woven into the hearts of His people: There's deep satisfaction that comes when we give away our possessions, which will fade, for the sake of people.

A HEART OF GENEROSITY

So how do we get a heart like this? How can we be among those who sow now in order to celebrate the harvest on the day our Lord returns?

Well, we all know the story of Ebeneezer Scrooge. The man had a ton of money, a stingy heart, and no friends. Did he change his mind on his own? No. Supernatural entities had to harass him all night long before he realized it would be a waste of life to die alone. It is better to die with an empty bank account and a packed funeral.

How do we get this heart of generosity? Jesus called the rich young man to give away his wealth and follow Him, and the young man would not do it. In response, Jesus uttered the famous line,

> **"Again I tell you, it is easier for a camel to go through the eye of a needle than for a rich person to enter the kingdom of God"** **(Matthew 19:24).**

Jesus' words shocked the disciples. Then who can get in?

Jesus responded:

> **"With man this is impossible, but with God all things are possible"** **(v. 26).**

Like Scrooge, you and I both need the supernatural to swoop in and change our hearts as well. But we don't need three ghosts; we need one man, the God-man, Jesus Christ.

Jesus came to this earth and accumulated no wealth. He never owned a home. He died without a single possession. But He changed all of human history. He gave everything for us—even His very life. When you fix your eyes on Him, He will lead you to care about others as He does.

The stingiest man in the New Testament, Zacchaeus, became one of the most generous after a single meal with Jesus.

> **"Zacchaeus stood and said to the Lord, 'Behold, Lord, the half of my goods I give to the poor. And if I have defrauded anyone of anything, I restore it fourfold.' And Jesus said to him, 'Today salvation has come to this house, since he also is a son of Abraham. For the Son of Man came to seek and to save the lost'" (Luke 19:8-10).**

Jesus Christ can change you too. So trust Him. Ask Him to give you a generous heart. Believe His Word. Know that He is coming. And join in His purposes for God's glory and our good.

APPLY TO LIFE

> **REFLECT:** Write down the top five things in your life that consume your thoughts most. Does your list include people or things? Consider how you can take steps now to show that all five top priorities are God and His people.

> **STUDY:** Do a concordance search of the word *money* to see what else the Bible has to say about finances.

> **LISTEN:** Purchase "This Is Not the End" by Gungor and "Sing Along" by Christy Nockels from the *This Changes Everything* playlist. Add these to your regular mix of music this week to remind you to keep your eyes focused on Jesus.

NOTES

THE PRAYER OF FAITH

> "Is anyone among you suffering? Let him pray. Is anyone cheerful? Let him sing praise. Is anyone among you sick? Let him call for the elders of the church, and let them pray over him, anointing him with oil in the name of the Lord. And the prayer of faith will save the one who is sick, and the Lord will raise him up. And if he has committed sins, he will be forgiven. Therefore, confess your sins to one another and pray for one another, that you may be healed. The prayer of a righteous person has great power as it is working."
>
> James 5:13-16

When I was in high school, if a Bible study leader ever said the words, "Tonight we're going to talk about prayer," my instinctual response would have been, *No. Tonight I am going to fall asleep until this is over.* Let's be honest—it doesn't initially sound like the most exciting topic.

Then I got to college. At some point I felt the need to incorporate more prayer into my life. So I signed up for the "24-hour prayer watch" at my church. The program called for individuals to commit to praying during a specific hour every week, with the goal that the church would have people praying during every hour of the day. I chose the 11:00 p.m. Sunday night shift.

The first week I decided to kneel beside my bed for the hour. (Kneeling is spiritual, right?) I interceded on behalf of my friends, my school, this nation, the world—I covered it all. Then I peeked at the clock. It had been three minutes. *Man, what am I supposed to do for an hour?* I fell asleep praying.

The next week I decided to pray in my closet. (Didn't Jesus say something about that being a good thing?) I didn't even make it to three minutes that time. The closet was just too warm and cozy!

By week three, I wasn't feeling like I was winning at this deal. I decided to begin taking walks with God. Then I found that the only way I could actually focus on talking to God was to talk out loud. As I walked around the neighborhood, I was surprised no one called the cops—a young man walking past homes talking in an animated fashion to no one. Finally I settled on praying at the local football stadium. I would sit up in the bleachers and tell God everything in my heart. Then I would look down and be shocked that an hour had flown by. I found that I began to look forward to that hour. My stress melted away, and my patience grew. Requests were answered in amazing ways. What at first sounded like a chore, I discovered, became a source of immense significance in my life.

As we close out this study in the Book of James, the brother of Jesus wants us to enjoy the powerful privilege we have of communing with the Almighty. He referred to prayer eight times in just eight verses! James understood that we may not fully grasp the purpose or the mechanics of prayer. When do we pray? What do we pray about? Does prayer really work? What about faith-healing? James has answers. Let's dive in.

What comes to mind when you think about prayer?

When do you pray?

What do you normally pray about?

Watch the *This Changes Everything* video for Session 8, available at *threadsmedia.com/thischangeseverything*.

WHEN DO WE PRAY?

Paul would often end his epistles by calling people to pray. He encouraged the Ephesians to "pray in the Spirit on all occasions with all kinds of prayers and requests" (Ephesians 6:18, NIV). He called the Thessalonians to "pray without ceasing, give thanks in all circumstances" (1 Thessalonians 5:17-18a). At the end of his book, James did a similar thing. Yet unlike Paul, who simply encouraged prayer in "all circumstances," James points out three particular situations that warrant prayer.

Situation 1: Feeling Bad?

"Is anyone among you suffering? Let him pray" (James 5:13a).

The word *suffering* in Greek is a combination of two words: *experience* and *bad*. So James begins this section by asking, "Are you experiencing anything bad?" James has mentioned all manner of difficult scenarios in his letter: persecution for your faith (5:10), economic woes (5:4), relational drama (4:1-12), enduring trials (1:2-4), and battling temptation (1:13-17). Experiencing any of these? James prescribes the proper response: pray.

James is quite clear that any form of suffering should lead us to pray. Yet for so many of us, when we encounter hardships, prayer isn't our automatic reaction. We convince ourselves that we can handle it on our own or we think, *God doesn't want to bother with that.* But the Bible says when we experience any kind of bad thing, we need to talk to God about it.

Think of a recent bad day. What was your instinctual response to difficulty?

Why do you think we are reticent to take our problems to God?

 The Greek word James used, *proseucesqw*, is the most common word for prayer used in the New Testament.

I remember reading about a debate between two ministers. One of them was a guy who thought we don't just cavalierly approach God with everything in our lives—God is so glorious that we should not presume that we may go rushing into His throne room with all of our petty problems. His defining metaphor was that God is like the president of the United States. You don't just throw open the door and run up and start telling the president about all your struggles. The other minister, who disagreed, cut him off and said, "Yes you do. You run in and interrupt the president with your problems when you are his kid. If you're his little son or daughter, you have direct access to the Oval Office. And everyone's going to let you run in because that's not just the president. He's also dad."

No matter our problem, God wants to commune with us. He is our Father, who sent His Son, Jesus Christ, to connect to each of us. Jesus endured everything we've been through. As Hebrews says, He is a sympathetic High Priest, so don't be shy.

> **"Let us then with confidence draw near to the throne of grace, that we may receive mercy and find grace to help in time of need"** (Hebrews 4:16).

George Müller, a great minister of the faith, opened an orphanage in Bristol, England in 1836. He didn't know how he would afford to care for all the children, but he trusted God to provide. George's wife was very sick and ended up dying of fever. It was a very difficult time for him, but he was always a very peaceful man. Somebody once asked him why he began the orphanage. He replied,

> "The first and primary object of the Institution was, and still is, that God might be magnified by the fact that the Orphans under my care were, and are, provided with all they need only by prayer and faith, without anyone being asked by me or my fellow-laborers, whereby it might be seen that God is faithful still and hears prayer still."[1]

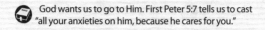 God wants us to go to Him. First Peter 5:7 tells us to cast "all your anxieties on him, because he cares for you."

George Müller was said to refer often to Psalm 55 to navigate all the tragedy he had faced and the kids for whom he was responsible:

> **"Cast your burden on the LORD,**
> **and he will sustain you"** (v. 22a).

When has God sustained you during a difficult time in the past?

How can you take comfort that He'll deliver you in the future?

This leads to a natural question, "What should we *say* when we talk to God about our suffering?" Should we pray for God to take our troubles away? Yes! Jesus did so before He faced the horrendous suffering of the cross.

> **"Then he said to them, 'My soul is very sorrowful, even to death; remain here, and watch with me.' And going a little farther he fell on his face and prayed, saying, 'My Father, if it be possible, let this cup pass from me; nevertheless, not as I will, but as you will.' And he came to the disciples and found them sleeping. And he said to Peter, 'So, could you not watch with me one hour? Watch and pray that you may not enter into temptation. The spirit indeed is willing, but the flesh is weak.' Again, for the second time, he went away and prayed, 'My Father, if this cannot pass unless I drink it, your will be done'"** (Matthew 26:38-42).

What can we learn from Jesus' prayer about how to approach God with our suffering?

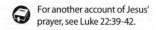 For another account of Jesus' prayer, see Luke 22:39-42.

Jesus prayed that if there was any way out of the cross, He was open to it. It is OK to ask God to remove the trials in our lives. Yet notice that He does not stop there. He recognized He was subject to God's will, praying that His will would be done despite the costs.

Even in His prayer, Jesus understood that God purposes pain for His will. The fact that Jesus prayed is the most persuasive reason we should pray. If the Son of God needed and used this resource, how can we hope to experience victory over difficult situations without it?

When we face trials, we are not meant only to pray, "Get me out, get me out!" We also pray to ask God for perspective in the moment. As we learned from James 1, when we face trials, we need to ask God for His sovereign guidance in the midst of our pain.

> **"If any of you lacks wisdom, let him ask God, who gives generously to all without reproach, and it will be given him" (v. 5).**

When we're suffering—in the middle of family issues, financial struggles, health battles, hard decisions, and overwhelming circumstances—no matter what it is, our response should be to cast our cares upon Him.

Where in your life do you need God's help to persevere patiently?

How can prayer give you wisdom in the midst of trials?

Situation 2: Feeling Good?
The next call to prayer in James 5:13 applies to those who are cheerful.

 Jesus prayed for various reasons—when He was tired from ministering to the needs of the crowd (Mark 1:35) and when He was concerned about the welfare of His disciples (John 17:6-19).

THIS CHANGES EVERYTHING

"Is anyone cheerful? Let him sing praise" (James 5:13b).

I love that James doesn't stop at praying during hard times. He swings around to the other side and says, "Is anyone (literally) feeling good?" Then sing! He uses an emotional word, which in the Greek is *psalleto*. The word's meaning transitioned from plucking a string (like in a harp), to making music, to singing. By James's day, the word meant to sing songs of praise to God. He uses a present-tense form of the verb, which means to act continuously.

Don't just sing. If you're happy and you know it, then keep on singing! That may mean pulling out an old favorite worship CD and cranking it up. As you're driving along, go ahead and sing it out. When people drive by and think you're crazy, roll down your window and ask them to join you. James tells us, *Are you happy? Then tell God all about it.*

Prayers of praise are sprinkled throughout the New Testament as writers paused to honor God for His remarkable goodness. We don't want to have a prayer life where we only speak to God when we're in trouble. Praise prayers help us become more aware of God's daily blessings.

What reasons do you have to be cheerful to God?

Occasionally, my wife, Donna, and I will just sit down on our couch and talk. I remember one night in particular when we had been talking through what was going on in our day, conversations we had, people we talked to, and we suddenly realized three hours had passed. We didn't watch a movie or anything. For a moment it surprised us. Then we thought, *You know, this actually makes a lot of sense. We should sit down and just talk about life with the one we love.*

It's the same with our God. He cares for us. He's our King, our Shepherd, our Friend, and the Lover of our soul. Our natural response should be to talk with Him.

 When Peter was in prison, everyone gathered and they prayed for his release. An angel of the Lord soon rescued him (see Acts 12:5-17).

Evaluate how well you're cultivating your relationship with God. How are you succeeding? What needs improvement?

I had some friends once who were moving into a new house. I saw them as they were looking around the house in the early stages, and one of the first things they did was find a closet and say, "Oh! This'll make a great prayer closet." And I said to myself, *I have never thought that in my life.* Usually we're thinking, *Where's my bed going to go? What color should I paint the walls?* They were thinking, *Where am I gonna pray here?*

How can you incorporate more focused conversation time with God into your daily life?

Situation 3: Prayers for the Sick and Sinful
Where the earlier types of prayers could be expressed individually or in groups, the next prayer is expressly communal.

> **"Is anyone among you sick? Let him call for the elders of the church, and let them pray over him, anointing him with oil in the name of the Lord" (v. 14).**

The word translated "sick" is used to apply to all manner of situations in the New Testament. It can describe limited mental capacity (Romans 6:19), spiritual weakness (Romans 5:6), or a weak conscience (1 Corinthians 8:7,9). This has led some to believe that James uses the term here to refer to those who are "spiritually weak," lacking faith in God or struggling with sin. Yet the word most often is used to describe physical illness. That seems to fit the context here.

Sometimes, if we're really sick, we need to call on the elders—spiritually mature church leaders—to pray over us. Simply put, there are some issues that we shouldn't be praying about on our own.

 For ideas on how to pray constantly, read the article "Living on a Prayer: Incorporating God Into Your Every Moment" at *threadsmedia.com.*

THIS CHANGES EVERYTHING

I have experienced this in my own life. When I broke my femur several years ago, a group of elders visited me in the hospital. They gathered around, put oil on me, and prayed for me. I don't know if I can fully explain the power in having the representatives of our church come around me to beg God to heal me. I hope all of you will immerse yourselves in churches and ministries where you can pray for one another like this.

Now some may say, "Wait a minute, why if I'm really sick would I call the elders to pray for me? Why wouldn't I call for the healers? Doesn't 1 Corinthians 12 talk about people with the gift of healing? Aren't there certain people who have special healing powers? Why doesn't James say, 'bring the healers in'? Why does he tell us to call for the elders?" This touches down on a popular, and often controversial, topic in the church today. How does healing work? Does God heal today? Does God raise up healers?

THE GIFT OF HEALING
In 1 Corinthians 12, Paul discussed gifts of healing.

> **"Now there are varieties of gifts, but the same Spirit; and there are varieties of service, but the same Lord; and there are varieties of activities, but it is the same God who empowers them all in everyone. To each is given the manifestation of the Spirit for the common good. For to one is given through the Spirit the utterance of wisdom, and to another the utterance of knowledge according to the same Spirit, to another faith by the same Spirit, to another gifts of healing by the one Spirit, to another the working of miracles, to another prophecy, to another the ability to distinguish between spirits, to another various kinds of tongues, to another the interpretation of tongues. All these are empowered by one and the same Spirit, who apportions to each one individually as he wills" (vv. 4-11).**

There are multiple giftings, and God hands them out for the common good. If we continued reading through 1 Corinthians 12, it gives us a physical analogy:

 Prayer was to accompany an anointing with olive oil. This practice served two purposes. First, oil was one of the main medicinal treatments in the first century. A second purpose was religious. Oil was regularly used in ceremonial anointing as a symbol of blessing.

We're all different parts of the body—some of us are like a foot, while others of us are like a hand. God has gifted different people in different ways, and we all need each other. One of us is not better than the other; we all work together to accomplish His mission.

Paul continues:

> "And God has appointed in the church first apostles, second prophets, third teachers, then miracles, then gifts of healing, helping, administrating, and various kinds of tongues. Are all apostles? Are all prophets? Are all teachers? Do all work miracles? Do all possess gifts of healing?" (vv. 28-30a).

Notice, Paul indicates that there are some in the believing community who are participating in these "gifts of healing." So is everyone healing? No. It seems that in the early church there were differences in the extent to which miraculous healings were manifest. Romans 12 and Ephesians 4 have very different gift lists, and healings and miracles never show up!

Yet are there some who participate in powerful works of healing? Yes! But let me say that we must be careful neither to despise nor exalt too highly those who participate in these sorts of things. A few biblical guardrails will help us from veering too far into condemning, or overly honoring those who partici-pate in healing.

1. If someone is used by God to help heal another person, that's not indicative of a special connection to God.
If you saw a minister participate in a miraculous healing of another person, would you assume he had a special connection with God? Both Jesus and Paul would caution you on that assessment! Both tell us that false prophets will do signs and wonders to lead people astray (see 2 Thessalonians 2:9; Matthew 24:24; Revelation 13:14; 16:14; 19:20). I have met people in the past who, based on their participation in a miraculous event of some kind, believe they have special insight into God. But miracles alone do not impress me. Jesus said the false prophets could do that stuff. Ministers should always be evaluated

 The picture James paints is of the elders praying "over" them and the person "rising up" from bed (vv. 14-15).

THIS CHANGES EVERYTHING

on the two things that marked Jesus' life and ministry: He was "full of grace and truth" (John 1:14,17). This naturally leads us to the second point.

2. Giftings of healings are never for self-exaltation but always for love.

In 1 Corinthians 12:7 it's clear that if God gives us some sort of gifting, it is for the common good. It's meant to help the community. Gifts that are more charismatic can easily become the basis for pride, just like teaching or preaching can. But they are meant to be an expression of love. In 1 Corinthians 13 Paul says, "if I have all faith, so as to remove mountains, but have not love, I am nothing" (v. 2b). For Paul, possession of gifts from the Spirit was never the main thing. What matters is love. I've met people who seem to be fixated upon wanting to see signs and wonders and to participate in the spectacular because they believe it would be cool or make their faith stronger. If this is you, be careful. Paul said you could have all this, but if you lack love, you have nothing.

What we should earnestly desire is that Christ would be honored through our self-sacrificing love for others. The greatest need is not to have gifts; it is to care for the sick—those sick with sin, sick with emotional disorders, sick with physical disease, and often a tangled mix of all three. The greatest miracle is that our hearts begin to care more about the lostness and pain of others than we do about our own comfort. So gifts are for the sake of love!

3. Only God can heal at will.

Nowhere in the Bible does it talk about "healers" or of a particular person possessing *the* gift of healing. In 1 Corinthians 12:9,28, Paul describes "the gifts of healing." This suggests what Paul refers to is that at different times for different illnesses God gives individuals various "gifts of healing." So you might find yourself drawn to pray for someone and see that person healed. Then at other times you may pray for someone else and healing not occur. This was the apostle Paul's experience.

God gave Paul the grace to heal the crippled man in Lystra (Acts 14:10), many people in Ephesus (Acts 19:12), a demonized girl in Philippi (Acts 16:18), and Eutychus, who died after falling out of a window (Acts 20:9-10).

But Paul couldn't heal himself from the ailment that he had when he preached in Galatia (Galatians 4:13-14). And evidently he couldn't heal Timothy from his stomach ailments (1 Timothy 5:23), Epaphroditus from his life-threatening sickness (Philippians 2:26-27), or Trophimus whom he left "sick at Miletus" (2 Timothy 4:20, HCSB). So sometimes God gave Paul gifts of healing and sometimes He didn't. Ultimately it's God's decision.

In certain communities at certain times God will give a gift of a healing. Then another place He'll give a different gift of a different healing. God apportions healings as He wills. There's not one person who has a gift of healing that they just use wherever they want. God alone can heal people, and He can use people, instrumentally, to do that.

4. Praying for healing is not wrong or bad.
Now some people are so wary of the scary, weird faith-healing crowd that they do not pray for God to do a mighty work of healing in their midst. That's crazy! We should ask God to heal! Yet healing should never become the focal point of the church. Paul made this clear to the Corinthians, who were tempted to become arrogant in showing off their spiritual gifts. He called teaching a greater gift. And he called love the greatest thing a community can possess. So pray for healing, but do not obsess over it. What matters to God is a community that is filled with love and truth.

So when James calls for prayer for the sick, he encourages the community to fall in line behind the Elders. These leaders of the church are selected based on spiritual maturity (Titus 1:5-9). As leaders of the church they are meant to guide the people of God in the usage of their gifts for the building up of the body (Ephesians 4:11-16). Here, the elders are meant to take the lead in praying for those in need, and the church joyfully follows her leaders (James 5:16).

How do you use your abilities and gifts to build up God's people?

 Elders in the New Testament collected money, resolved theological conflict, prayed for and anointed the sick, and shepherded congregations (see Acts 11:29; 14:23; 15:2; 20:28; 21:17-26; Titus 1:6-9; and 1 Timothy 3:1-7).

THIS CHANGES EVERYTHING

What comfort can you find in the knowledge that healing is solely in God's hands?

How does that strengthen your resolve to pray for healing? To understand God's will?

WHEN HEALING DOESN'T HAPPEN

Now the next verse has a bit of controversy attached to it as well! James 5:15 seems to contain an unconditional promise of healing.

> **"And the prayer of faith will save the one who is sick, and the Lord will raise him up" (v. 15a).**

For every story of miraculous healing, we have a story of those who continue to suffer despite their petitions to God. What's the explanation? Some people will argue that what James was talking about only worked with the apostles—that this kind of healing doesn't occur anymore. However, James isn't talking about the apostles. He's discussing elders in our churches.

Others will say God will heal either physically in that moment of prayer, or that believers will find ultimate healing with God in eternity when they die. While that's true, we wouldn't need the elders to anoint the sick with oil for that. So that's not really what James is saying.

Another group will look at this text and argue that a person wasn't healed because his or her faith failed. We'll hear about healers who will say stuff like, "Well, you were sick. You came to me to pray for you. You stayed sick, so the reason is you didn't have enough faith." Yet even the most faithful Christians will suffer at times even when covered with prayer.

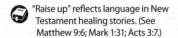 "Raise up" reflects language in New Testament healing stories. (See Matthew 9:6; Mark 1:31; Acts 3:7.)

So what are we to believe? Let's go back to James 4:

"If the Lord wills, we will live and do this or that" (v. 15b).

When James said, "the prayer of faith will save" (5:15), he wasn't giving us an unconditional mechanical formula for healing: "If you do X and Y, then Z will happen." James was saying that we offer a prayer "of faith." Faith in the God who determines whether we live or do this or that! We must not make the mistake of reading James 5:15 without the context of James 4:15.

We trust the God who holds our lives in His hands. But does this acknowledgment of His rule over our lives mean we shouldn't pray? No! God loves to do the miraculous. He loves to use means. He delights to hear the prayers of His people and answer them, often in amazing ways!

FAITH AND PHYSICAL HEALING

Ben Sherwood, a Harvard grad, Rhodes Scholar at Oxford, and successful producer both at ABC's "Good Morning America" then NBC's Nightly News, wrote a book about survival. Some of his findings are intuitive. Young, physically fit men survive plane crashes more than elderly, infirm women. Others are less obvious. People who are left-handed die much younger than people who are right-handed. People with bad initials also die sooner than those with positive initials. I'm a lefty with the initials BS—according to his book, I'm a goner.

As he was writing, he thought he should include a chapter on faith, but admittedly, he didn't want to. He said,

> "When I started writing this book, I was somewhat skeptical of the role of faith in survival. . . . But as I began to interview survivors around the world, I noticed a remarkable pattern. . . . As many as 75 or 80 percent cited a higher power as an important reason for their survival."[2]

So he realized he needed to investigate this phenomena.

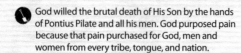 God willed the brutal death of His Son by the hands of Pontius Pilate and all his men. God purposed pain because that pain purchased for God, men and women from every tribe, tongue, and nation.

THIS CHANGES EVERYTHING

In his book *The Survivors Club,* Ben tells the story of 21-year-old Gary McCane Jr. Gary was working on the air-conditioning and heating of a new home in Woodmont, Kentucky, when someone came running up saying that two workers were trapped in a nearby, underground cistern. He volunteered to shimmy down the hole and rescue them. As he started down, there was a huge explosion in the underground tank. It lit Gary on fire. He climbed out and extinguished the flames. Gary had "third-degree burns on 85 percent of his body."[3] The book continues:

> "He spent the next two and a half months in a medically induced coma, undergoing forty surgeries. . . . He still remembers a vivid dream . . . He saw himself walking down a sterile hallway, passing a nursing station, and arriving at the exit. In his dream, he tried to open the double doors but they wouldn't budge, so he returned to his room. Later, he found out that his grandfather—known as Pappaw—had gathered a group of . . . ministers to pray in the waiting room. On the night that Gary had 'coded'—hospital-speak for cardiac arrest—Pappaw and his friends had laid hands on the exit of the hospital. They asked God to help Gary heal before he left the burn unit. In a coma, of course, he had no way of knowing the layout of the hospital, including the location of the nursing station, hallway, and doors. And yet his dream was accurate in every detail. . . . Gary's recovery was so quick that he was released from the hospital one year before the doctors had predicted."[4]

So here's the author, Ben Sherwood, who's not a Christian, telling the story about elders who came and prayed for this guy who was healed. Does God heal? Absolutely. So we should approach Him with our physical ailments. Yet notice that James' concern is not only for our body. Our sickness may be spiritual as well.

How do you respond to these statements?

When have you experienced healing or seen it in a loved one? When have you seen someone who hasn't been healed?

FAITH AND SPIRITUAL HEALING

There's a spiritual component, too, because James 5 also talks about forgiveness.

"And if he has committed sins, he will be forgiven" (v. 15b).

In the ancient world, sin and sickness were often tied together. Yet notice that James says "if" he has committed sins. The story of Job teaches us that we cannot draw a direct link between illness and sin (Job 1:1,8,22; 2:3). Jesus affirms this as well (John 9:2-3). So if we're sick, we can't automatically blame it on sin. And yet the Bible does recognize that often a connection exists between sin and sickness.

In 1 Corinthians 11, we have this disturbing passage about the Corinthians getting drunk during communion. Paul warns them that they're getting sick and dying because of their sin toward "the body and blood of the Lord" (vv. 27-30).

So not all sickness is caused by sin. Yet sin and sickness, spiritual health and physical wellness are linked. Interestingly, modern scientific studies support this clear biblical teaching!

Time magazine published an article called "The Biology of Belief." It was a secular discussion on how faith relates to healing.

> "Here's what's surprising: a growing body of scientific evidence suggests that faith may indeed bring us health. People who attend religious services do have a lower risk of dying in any one year than people who don't attend. People who believe in a loving God fare better after a diagnosis of illness than people

who believe in a punitive God. No less a killer than AIDS will back off at least a bit when it's hit with a double-barreled blast of belief. 'Even accounting for medications,' says Dr. Gail Ironson, a professor of psychiatry and psychology at the University of Miami who studies HIV and religious belief, 'spirituality predicts for better disease control.'"[5]

The article goes on to discuss how all these scientists from Duke, Miami, and Ohio have been researching the relationship of faith and prayer to healing—and they're realizing there's a direct link we can't deny. They're finding the people who endure health problems better are those who have a theology of God that's big enough to encompass even pain.

Another study at the University of Texas in Austin reveals that those who go to church regularly—that is, once a week, on average through a human being's life—will live 7 years longer than those who don't go to church. Isn't that an interesting number? If you go to church once a week, you'll live roughly 7 years longer than somebody who doesn't. More specifically, what researchers found is if you go to church once a week, you're likely to live 6.6 years longer. And if you attend worship more than once a week, your advantage is 7.6 years.[6] It's amazing that all these different people—religious and secular—are finding out that a strong connection exists between the spiritual and the physical.

James acknowledges this connection, and he affirms that the best remedy for our infirmities may be confession of our sin!

> **"Therefore, confess your sins to one another and pray for one another, that you may be healed. The prayer of a righteous person has great power as it is working"** (James 5:16).

The guilt of our sin can become a crushing weight in our souls. Again, prayer is the proper prescription. King David in the Old Testament experienced this phenomenon. David committed serious sins, such as murder and adultery. He expressed well the relief one experiences after being freed from the burden of sin and guilt.

"Blessed is the one whose transgression is forgiven,
   whose sin is covered.
Blessed is the man against whom the LORD counts no
   iniquity, and in whose spirit there is no deceit.
For when I kept silent, my bones wasted away
   through my groaning all day long.
For day and night your hand was heavy upon me;
   my strength was dried up as by the heat of summer.
Selah
I acknowledged my sin to you,
   and I did not cover my iniquity;
I said, 'I will confess my transgressions to the LORD,'
   and you forgave the iniquity of my sin" (Psalm 32:1-5).

Maybe you're wrestling with some dark things that you've never told a soul. Maybe you're struggling with depression or lack of energy. Maybe you're just feeling guilty that you haven't made enough time for God lately.

The spiritual, physical, and emotional wires in our lives are all crossed. Sometimes it's hard to know which one's to blame, but they're all linked. When we're lacking joy, vibrancy, and even energy, it could be because we're not right with God. But the God who delights to heal also delights to forgive. Yet, just as the prayer for physical healing was best performed in community, so James calls us to pursue spiritual healing in community. We were meant to confess our sins to one another, and pray for one another, that we might be healed. Some of you have asked God for years to forgive you of particular sins in your life. Let me tell you, He has forgiven you if you have trusted in Christ. Yet you have not experienced the joy of freedom. You need community for that. James calls for confession of sin in the context of the believing community. As they say in A.A., "You are only as sick as your secrets."

SEEKING ACCOUNTABILITY

In every town I live in, one of the first things I do is to ask God to show me someone I can pray with and confess my sins to. When I moved to College Station, Texas, I started making a list during my quiet time of potential accountability partners.

Oddly enough, the people at the top of my list never make it. At one point I was like, *This is the guy,* and then a month later he moved. So then, after meeting with a local minister, I thought, *Lord, maybe he's the guy.* We spent some time together, and we were talking about our interests. He said, "I am just passionate about gardening." I remember internally going, *Yeah, I don't think we're going to be close.* Fast-forward a few years, and he has become one of my closest friends in town. We confess everything to each other. We pray for each other, and God uses that. It's a great thing, not just spiritually, but emotionally and even physically.

Some of us have been carrying burdens we were never meant to carry alone. That doesn't mean to shout it out on your favorite social media site or to tell it to your entire circle of friends, but it does mean careful confession to God and to another person in an authentic, God-honoring relationship.

We have a God who loves to heal and forgive. We should be confessing our sins to each other, utilizing the community of faith that God gave us. We should be doing life together, helping one another with our struggles, and praying for one another that we might be healed.

Name one person you can be honest with about your struggles and mistakes. How does that person give you encouragement and perseverance for the road ahead?

If you don't currently have an accountability partner, take a moment to pray. Ask God to reveal to you whom you could talk to and pray with for healing.

As a general rule, you don't need to confess your sins to people of the opposite gender. That kind of authenticity opens the door to further struggles and heartache.

ONE IS THE LONELIEST NUMBER

There's a movie I watched a couple years ago called *The Bridge*. It's all about how the Golden Gate Bridge is the number one destination for people who commit suicide. The video asserts that many suicidal people are drawn to the bridge because they carry romantic notions of boldly leaping into the beyond.

A coroner report I read confirms this is actually not true. A person who jumps off the bridge falls approximately 245 feet in four seconds. It shatters bones, throws shrapnel into organs, and causes extensive internal bleeding. Then the person descends 40 feet under water, and in excruciating pain, drowns or asphyxiates.[7] The coroner said normally a corpse is stiff like a board. However, for those who jump off the bridge, they're like a sack of pellets because they've destroyed their interior structure. Why am I telling you all that detail? Because of a 19-year-old kid named Kevin Hines.

Kevin was bipolar but didn't know it at the time. All he knew was there was a constant voice in his head telling him he was a loser. One day he finally believed that voice and decided to kill himself. Kevin tells the most tragic story of standing on the bridge for 40 minutes trying to send out the "somebody ask me how I'm doing or make eye contact with me" vibe.

> "No one approached him to ask what was wrong. When a tourist came up and asked whether he could take her photo, Hines said that was the final straw—clear proof that no one cared. He took the picture, then jumped. Instantly, he realized he had made a mistake, and came up with a plan to save his life.
>
> 'It was simply this: God, save me, A. B, throw your head back. C, hit feet first,' Hines said. 'And I did all of that.'"[8]

Kevin asked the God whom he'd blown off his whole life for help. He hit the water at 75 miles an hour, maintaining consciousness.[9] Kevin realized he wasn't dead but that both his legs were broken so he would drown. As he started to pray, Kevin felt a bump on his leg that he soon realized was keeping him on the surface. The bump turned out to be a sea lion that kept him afloat until the Coast Guard found him.[10] Where's Kevin now? He prays with people at the

 If you're searching for someone you can trust, check out *Mentor: How Along-the-Way Discipleship Will Change Your Life* by Chuck Lawless at *threadsmedia.com/mentor*.

Golden Gate Bridge who think they want to jump and speaks across the country about suicide and mental health, particularly within the military sector.[11]

Isn't that crazy? God loves good stories. Will He let us die? Yes. We're all going to die, 100 percent guaranteed. Yet God loves to work miracles. He loves to forgive people of sin. He loves to rescue people who are at rock bottom, in the darkest places, or sailing into oblivion.

If you cry out for help, God loves to say yes. That's the kind of God we have. Look to a God who loves to respond. He may not always answer the way you want, but He will always listen and care.

Who around you needs some encouragement? What's stopping you from reaching out?

How can investing in others bring forgiveness, healing, and new life?

THE GREATEST RESCUE OF ALL

The closing verses of the Book of James don't sound very traditional, yet they are important. The person who strays from the truth is a Christian who has neglected his faith, one who needs spiritual restoration. The ministry of restoration includes a fellow Christian who turns him back. This action involves a gracious but determined spirit.

> **"My brothers, if anyone among you wanders from the truth and someone brings him back, let him know that whoever brings back a sinner from his wandering will save his soul from death and will cover a multitude of sins" (vv. 19-20).**

 If you or someone you know is struggling with suicidal thoughts, call the National Suicide Prevention Lifeline at 1.800.273.TALK (8255).

James closes his book discussing those caught in sin. When we see someone in sin, we may get to be a part of God's saving grace by being the voice that helps pull that person back from death. He may be on a trajectory and in a sinful lifestyle that will absolutely cause the end of his life and you could rescue him. That's what Kevin is now doing on the bridge. That's what we can do wherever we're planted.

Sometimes the person caught in sin may be the one looking back in the mirror. Greater than any healing we've discussed so far is the salvation God affords to those who don't know Him. The Bible says that we are all sinners. We have all fallen short of the glory of God. God made us to be something glorious and to appreciate His glory. Through His mercy, God brought us a solution.

That's where we need to spend our days: calling our attention toward something glorious. In our sin, God sent someone to rescue us, His own Son. It was Jesus Christ who came to this earth to live a perfect life that we could not. He died the death we deserved, and then extended His arms toward us and says, "everyone who lives and believes in me shall never die" (John 11:26).

Reconciliation with God can happen to anybody no matter how dark, broken, or twisted our lives may have become. God releases His power in our lives through our prayers in ways we never fully understand. So my hope is that we will be people of prayer. We can look to His Son and ask for rescue, and He will answer. God listens to those who cry out to Him.

APPLY TO LIFE

> **REFLECT:** The example of Elijah in James 5:17-18 is important because he was a man with a nature like ours. He shared our potential for weakness. Yet even with this frail human nature he prayed faithfully and the results were powerful (1 Kings 17–18). God does not reserve His blessings and the power of prayer for a spiritually elite class. These blessings are available to all His children. Take time to consider Elijah's example and how that can influence your prayers this week.

> **STUDY:** For further study on the Book of James, listen to Ben Stuart's 2009 sermon series podcast on James, available on iTunes under "Breakaway Ministries." Also consider reading Douglas J. Moo's *The Letter of James, Pillar New Testament Commentary.*

> **LISTEN:** Purchase "Run" by Sanctus Real and "Find You on My Knees" by Kari Jobe from the *This Changes Everything* playlist. Add these to your regular mix of music this week to remind you to be a person of constant prayer.

NOTES

NOTES

NOTES

NOTES

SESSION 1

1. Hershel Shanks and Ben Witherington III, *The Brother of Jesus: The Dramatic Story & Meaning of the First Archaeological Link to Jesus & His Family* (New York: HarperCollins Publishers, 2003), 187.
2. N.T. Wright, "Part V: Belief, Event and Meaning," *The Resurrection of the Song of God: Christian Origins and the Question of God,* vol. 3 (Minneapolis: Fortress Press, 2003), 686.
3. See Eusebius, *Historia Ecclesiastica* 2.23.6.

SESSION 2

1. Norman Ollestad, *Crazy for the Storm: A Memoir of Survival* (New York: HarperCollins, 2009).
2. These insights were influenced from Tim Keller's sermons "Power for Facing Trouble," "Two Basic Kinds of Trouble," and "Benefits of Facing Trouble." You can hear these sermons from Keller and more at *http://sermons.redeemer.com/store/index.cfm*.
3. David Sheff, *Beautiful Boy: A father's journey through his son's addiction* (New York: Houghton Mifflin Company, 2008), 133.
4. Ibid., 256.
5. C. S. Lewis, *Readings for Meditation and Reflection* (New York: HarperCollins Publishers, 1992), 71.
6. Journal entry used by permission of the family.
7. "Baca," *Holman Bible Dictionary,* 144.

SESSION 3

1. Johnny Cash, *Cash: The Autobiography* (New York: HarperOne, 2003), 141, 152, 155.
2. Caitlin Flanagan, "Is There Hope for the American Marriage?" *Time* magazine, July 2, 2009. Available online at *www.time.com*.

SESSION 4

1. John Piper, sermon "Does James Contradict Paul?" from the series "Romans," The Greatest Letter Ever Written. You can hear Piper's sermon at *www.desiringGod.org*.

2. Augustus M. Toplady, "Rock of Ages, Cleft for Me," *The Baptist Hymnal* (Nashville: LifeWay Worship, 2008), hymn 463.

3. The author heard these four signs in the sermon "Life of Faith" in Tim Keller's series "James: A Faith that Comes Down to Earth." You can hear Keller's series at *http://sermons.redeemer.com/store/index.cfm*.

4. Adapted from a Jonathan Edwards's 1752 sermon "True Grace Distinguished From the Experience of Devils."

5. "Abraham," *Holman Bible Dictionary*, 10.

SESSION 5

1. "Energy Division Resolution E-4116 from the Public Utilities Commission of the State of California." Published September 20, 2007. Accessed February 8, 2013. Available online at *www.cpuc.ca.gov/puc*.

2. "Spurgeon's Service at Surrey Gardens," Church History Timeline, *Christianity. com*. Accessed January 25, 2013. Available online at *www.christianity.com*.

3. Richard John Knowling, *Epistle of Saint James* (London: Methuen & Co., 1904), 78.

SESSION 6

1. Jonathan Edwards, "The Memoirs of Jonathan Edwards," of *The Works of Jonathan Edwards, Vol. 1*, Edward Hickman, ed. (Banner of Truth Trust, 1974), lxii.

2. Stephen Mansfield, *The Faith of the American Soldier* (Lake Mary, FL: FrontLine, 2005), 5–6.

3. Ibid., 7–8.

4. For more details on this story, see chapter 12, "The Breaking Point," in Stephen E. Ambrose's book *Band of Brothers: E Company, 506th Regiment, 101st Airborne from Normandy to Hitler's Eagle's Nest*.

SESSION 7

1. Jean Jacques Rousseau, *The Confessions of Jean Jacques Rousseau,* vol. 2 of 3 (2007), 96.
2. Nachum Gabler, Charles Lammam, and Milagros Palacios, "Generosity in Canada and the United States: The 2012 Generosity Index." Fraser Institute. December 13, 2012. Accessed January 30, 2013. Available online at *www.fraserinstitute.org.*

SESSION 8

1. Basil Miller, *George Müller: Man of Faith and Miracles* (Minneapolis: Bethany House Publishers, 1941), 51.
2. Ben Sherwood, *The Survivors Club: The Secrets and Science that Could Save Your Life* (New York: Grand Central Publishing, 2009), 134.
3. Ibid., 100.
4. Ibid, 100–101.
5. Jeffrey Kluger, "The Biology of Belief," *Time* magazine, February 12, 2009. Accessed February 7, 2013. Available online at *www.time.com.*
6. 1999 University of Texas at Austin study, as quoted in Ben Sherwood, *The Survivors Club,* 139.
7. "LETHAL BEAUTY / No easy death: Suicide by bridge is gruesome, and death is almost certain. The fourth in a seven-part series on the Golden Gate Bridge barrier debate," *San Francisco Chronicle,* November 2, 2005. Accessed February 7, 2013. Available online at *www.sfgate.com.*
8. "Man Survives Suicide Jump from Golden Gate Bridge," "Good Morning America," April 28, 2006. Accessed February 7, 2013. Available online at *http://abcnews.go.com/GMA.*
9. "Kevin Hines Story," The Bridge Rail Foundation. Accessed February 5, 2013. Available online at *www.bridgerail.org.*
10. Ibid.
11. For more information on Kevin Hines, go to *www.kevinhinesstory.com.*

MORE BIBLE STUDIES

CREATION UNRAVELED
THE GOSPEL ACCORDING TO GENESIS
BY MATT CARTER AND HALIM SUH

The words we read in Genesis are the same words that provided hope for hungry Israelites in the wilderness, breathed courage into the heart of David, and fed the soul of Jesus Himself during His time on earth. God's promises are as relevant today as they were "in the beginning."

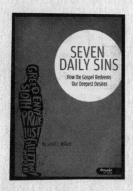

SEVEN DAILY SINS
HOW THE GOSPEL REDEEMS OUR DEEPEST DESIRES
BY JARED C. WILSON

The so-called seven deadly sins—lust, greed, envy, sloth, pride, gluttony, wrath—are not merely things we do but, as Jesus reveals, conditions of our heart. Even if we don't act on them, we carry these desires around every day. How does the gospel address the needs at the root of these sins and empower us to break patterns of bondage to them? *Seven Daily Sins* reveals from Scripture how Christians can experience freedom by the redemptive power of the gospel of Jesus.

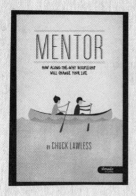

MENTOR
HOW ALONG-THE-WAY DISCIPLESHIP WILL CHANGE YOUR LIFE
BY CHUCK LAWLESS

Drawing from biblical examples like Jesus and His disciples, Paul, and Timothy, author Chuck Lawless explores the life-transforming process of a mentoring relationship. This study is both a practical and a spiritual guide to biblical mentoring, providing easy-to-model life application for how to have and be a mentor.

ENGAGE
A PRACTICAL GUIDE TO EVANGELISM
BY J. D. GREEAR, ROB TURNER, DERWIN GRAY, AND BEN REED

The simple truth of the gospel doesn't change. And while this truth is timeless, we must always evaluate the presentation of that truth to make sure it's connecting in a culturally relevant way. This practical study examines the act of sharing your faith. It answers questions like, How do you begin a conversation about Jesus? What if people have questions you're not sure how to answer? What do you say if they respond positively or if they reject God's message?

ORDINARY
HOW TO TURN THE WORLD UPSIDE DOWN
BY TONY MERIDA

The kingdom of God isn't coming with light shows and shock and awe, but with lowly acts of service performed during the normal rhythms of life. *Ordinary* encourages participants to move into a life of mission and justice— speaking up for the voiceless, caring for the single mom, restoring the broken, bearing burdens, welcoming the functionally fatherless, and speaking the good news to people on a regular basis in order to change the world..

EXPERIENCING GOD
GOD'S INVITATION TO YOUNG ADULTS
BY HENRY T. BLACKABY AND RICHARD BLACKABY

What Should I do with My life? How Can God Use me? Many of us ask those questions, but none more so than young adults. If you're searching for God's will and practical advice as you seek answers to important life decisions, *Experiencing God: God's Invitation to Young Adults* is for you. The goal of this Bible study is to teach you how to live your life in such a way that you'll experience everything God intends for your life. This will happen when you fully embrace God's invitation to live through Him.

GROUP CONTACT INFORMATION

Name _____ Number _____

Email _____

Name _____ Number _____

Email _____

Name _____ Number _____

Email _____

Name _____ Number _____

Email _____

Name _____ Number _____

Email _____

Name _____ Number _____

Email _____

Name _____ Number _____

Email _____

Name _____ Number _____

Email _____

Name _____ Number _____

Email _____

Name _____ Number _____

Email _____

Name _____ Number _____

Email _____